WRITE
YOUR BOOK IN A WEEK

PUBLISH
A HIGH-QUALITY BOOK IN SIX WEEKS

LAUNCH
YOUR BOOK AND BECOME AN
INTERNATIONAL AMAZON BEST SELLER

Insider Secrets to Accelerate Your Influence, Authority, and Impact with an Inspirational, Best-Selling Book

By
DAVE THOMPSON

Praise for Inspirational Book Writers (IBW)

Too many live their life and don't reach their full potential. That was definitely me until Dave and the IBW team inspired me to UNLEASH! The whole experience was totally life changing—transformational, in fact! From the conventional life-coaching approach to the unconventional nuances of heart and soul, IBW is "THE PLACE" to turn your dreams into reality.
Kelvin Holliday, Founder and Head Adventurer Transformational Group

The Inspirational Book Writers program is the perfect platform to get your ideas finally out to the world, and your book is by far the greatest business card you can ever design!
Daniel Tonkin, Entrepreneur and Author

IBW and Dave Thompson have been essential for my personal and professional dream to get a book written. Two years down the track and I have written five books with IBW and have eight more to easily smash out with this system! Love working with Dave.
Jean Sheehan, Director Millennium Education & International Speaker and Author

This book is for anyone that knows they are destined for greatness. As Dave says, most people want to play a big game, only a few actually do. This book is for the special individual that is claiming their greatness and sharing it with the world. If you have ever had an idea for a book, this book will lead you to action.

Matt Lavars, Founder, Relentless Education

Wow, I haven't stopped crying, you're speaking to my Soul.

Your book is Manna from heaven! A blend of Jedi mind powers with genius pearls of wisdom, and so many #TruthBombs. Ha! There is no way you can hide because Dave sees all the procrastination tactics, he knows them all! On a personal note, I've been the recipient of Dave's ability to hold delicious, grounded space, like a BOSS! Thank you for being a beautiful human. Arohanui.

Patty-Ann Waho, Intimacy Coach

Dave Thompson has a strategic mind that is nothing short of world class. His coaching ability to navigate the fastest solution to generate the result you want to create is truly spectacular.

In a 10-minute conversation, Dave helped me identify the key words to succinctly sum up the industry niche I'd just newly created. This has not only set the direction of my first book but transformed the conversation around my brand and business and opened up a world of opportunity.

Justine Davis, Director - Brand Magic

Dave Thompson's Inspirational Book Writers delivered on every promise. Need a creative and nurturing space to write in?—done. Need support, encouragement, collaboration, and challenge to turn your book from a mess of ideas into a finished book?—done. Need to know how to market and launch your book and become an Amazon best seller?—done. I always thought it would be hard to write and publish a book. It wasn't. It was far easier than I imagined and it's because Dave and his team made it that way.
Stacey Ashley, Award-Winning Coach, LinkedIn Top Voice, and Amazon Best-Selling Author of *The New Leader*

My experience with Dave and the team and IBW was world class. From start to finish, the program is skilfully designed to ensure participants move through the process of book writing with ease and confidence. If you want to write an amazing book in the shortest possible time with the backing of an experienced and supportive team, IBW is the program of choice.
Salena Kulkarni, CEO and Investment Advisor, Chartered Accountant

Books also by Dave Thompson

The Entrepreneurial Hero's Journey

Balance After Burnout

Inspirational Book Writing

Living Outrageously

The Book Writer Breakthrough

First published in 2020 by Dave Thompson
© Dave Thompson
The moral rights of the author have been asserted.
This book is an Inspirational Book Writers book.

Author:
   Thompson, Dave

Title:
   WRITE PUBLISH LAUNCH: Insider Secrets to Accelerate Your Influence, Authority, and Impact With an Inspirational, Best-Selling Book

ISBN:
   978-1-716-97957-6

All rights reserved. Except as permitted under the Australian Copyright Act 1968 (for example, a fair dealing for the purposes of study, research, criticism or review), no part of this book may be reproduced, stored in a retrieval system, communicated or transmitted in any form or by any means without prior written permission. All enquiries should be made to the publisher at writeabook@inspirationalbookwriters.com

Editor-in-chief: Anita Saunders
Cover Design: Sarah Rose Graphic Design

Disclaimer:
The material in this publication is of the nature of general comment only, and does not represent professional advice. It is not intended to provide specific guidance for particular circumstances and it should not be relied on as the basis for any decision to take action or not take action on any matter which it covers. Readers should obtain professional advice where appropriate, before making any such decision. To the maximum extent permitted by law, the author and publisher disclaim all responsibility and liability to any person, arising directly or indirectly from any person taking or not taking action based on the information in this publication.

Dedication

*To all of you out there taking action each day
to make the world a better place.*

Table of Contents

Note to the Readers xiii

Introduction—Where It All Began xix

Chapter 1—Before You Begin.. 1

Chapter 2—Getting Started With Purpose and Direction 15

Chapter 3—Write Your Book in a Week 45

Chapter 4—Publish a High-Quality Book 53

Chapter 5—Launch Your Book to International
Amazon Best Seller 67

What's Next?..103

The Online Book Writing Intensive 105

Publish + Launch 107

Note to the Readers

Dear Reader,

Thank you for being here. What you hold in your hands is a guidebook containing the accumulated wisdom of over half a decade's worth of inspirational books that have been written in a week. Since 2014, my business, Inspirational Book Writers, has worked with people from all over the world in almost every market you could imagine helping them write, publish, and launch an inspirational, best-selling book.

What this book is really about is handing you, in book form, EVERYTHING we have learnt about how to make the often painful process as easy and graceful as can be. I often say that writing a book is a lot like climbing Mount Everest—it is possible to do it, and many people do, but it is WAY easier with a guide to show you the way. So, consider this book your personal "Sherpa" in your own book writing journey.

The need for a book like this is self-evident. *Forbes* magazine reports that 81% of the population want to write a book, and yet every year, less than 0.1% achieve their goal. That means writing a book is something everyone wants to do, but hardly anyone does! That's because there are lots of pitfalls, many psychological traps, and hundreds of steps where often people have no idea how to get started. This book solves all of those problems and more.

This book is different from all the other books you'll find on book writing. Firstly, most other books in this space are written to "sell" you into their next book writing course or program. As such, you get a lot of the sizzle, and no sausage (or "essence of sausage," as someone once remarked to me!). This book is different though. The intention behind this book is not to "sell" you on our products and services. I'm confident that will happen naturally as you read the pages, and if what I'm saying resonates with you I invite you to reach out, because we can likely do some great work together on your book.

Second, and most importantly, this book focuses on the ideas, strategies, and steps you need to take to write your inspirational, best-selling book in a week. We have a specific solution, for a specific problem, for a specific type of book writer. It is NOT full of general, untested ideas. What you will find in this book are the exact things you will hear me coach my book writers on. You are getting the gold, direct from ground zero, where me and my team are in the trenches every day, doing the work. This is what is working RIGHT NOW for our clients.

Third, this book is different because it addresses the emotional journey of book writing. Like I said above, everyone wants to write a book, and every year hardly anyone succeeds, and the reason is because their emotions trap them. Fear, paralysed will, procrastination, impostor syndrome, writer's block—the list goes on. What you'll see in the "Write" section is that we orchestrate the book writing environment so that these emotional blocks cannot exist. To that end, this book could have easily been called *Flow State Book Writing*.

Most likely though, if you're holding this book in your hands or on your eBook reader, it's because you were attracted to the RESONANCE of this book. On an energetic, perhaps even soul level, something called out to you to be like "YES, THIS!" That's part of the magic of our books and what we aim for with all our clients—that not only is their book marketed in a powerful way, but that it is also encoded with a special "feeling" that attracts the reader.

We want your readers to be walking down the street past a bookstore, when suddenly they get a lightning bolt of inspiration to go into the store—back corner, shelf at eye-level—BOOM! There's your book. So yes, this is about practically and logically doing all the right things from a positioning and marketing perspective, AND making sure your book is BUZZING with the vibration that will attract your ideal clients.

So, who is this book for?

It's for inspirational people doing inspiring things in the world. The thing that unites all our book writers, regardless of background or topic, is that they have a unique talent, skill, or methodology, or an inspiring story that will solve people's problems, uplift their community, and raise the consciousness of the planet.

There are a lot of problems out there in the world, and people like you have the messages, insights, and wisdom that can make a big difference in your space. The world NEEDS your voice, because no-one can say it like you can. It's your unique way, that curious story that you tell in YOUR way—that's what's important.

So, if LEGACY, IMPACT, and GLOBAL CHANGE are important to you, you are in the right place.

Practically speaking, this book, and indeed the write-your-book-in-a-week method, has been specifically designed for coaches, consultants, speakers, and entrepreneurs. We built our entire program for you. We know you don't have six months to take out of your business to go to Bali and sit in your hut and write your memoirs, but we do know you can carve out one week to get something really important done.

If you're in personal growth, leadership, entrepreneurship, health, healing, education, relationships, spirituality, finance, wealth creation, or similar, then you're in the right place.

This book will guide you through our Write—Publish—Launch methodology. Getting started is often the hardest step to take, which is why we have designed a powerful, transformational process called the Book Map Game Plan to get you on track from the get-go. By having an effective Book Map Game Plan, you will potentially save yourself months and years of false starts by starting out on the right foot.

In "Write," you will discover how to access the Quantum Reality to get your book done in a week. This section alone is worth the price of the book. Once you really GET how to create rapidly and in flow, your book can pour out of you in a matter of HOURS. For real—I have seen people click into the Quantum Reality, and 12 hours later emerge with a complete book. I myself have written my last two books in 12 hours and 20 hours respectively. This book was completed in 28 hours of writing.

You'll also learn how to create an environment where procrastination, etc. literally cannot exist. I sometimes get people emailing me, saying, "Dave, how is it possible to write a book in a week?" When you read this section, it will all make sense and you'll be able to see how it is definitely possible.

In "Publish," you will learn the secrets to creating a high-quality book that you can be proud of. You will discover how to create a title and sub-title combination that is compelling, powerful, and enticing, and how to match that with a cover design that POPS out at the reader. We look at your publishing options, and how to best complete the review and refinement process with grace and ease. Publishing is a somewhat mechanical science, but also an art, as there are many little touches that can really take your book to a whole new level.

In "Launch," you will discover how to launch your book to #1 Amazon best seller in multiple categories (and perhaps too in multiple markets, becoming an international best seller). Launching is all about getting your book into the hands of the people who need it the most, while also building credibility and authority, and profiting at the same time. We will share with you our four-stage launch sequence that anyone can use (even if you have a small following) to create book launch success.

And finally, the other intention of this book is for it to be a resource for all our coaches, and clients, to guide you whenever you need to refocus. As you'll discover shortly, one big reason to write your book is to leverage your knowledge. When your ideas are accessible to everyone on the planet, it helps A LOT with getting your ideas to the world in a bigger and better way, without burning you out.

So please enjoy, and may this book give you the kick up the pants, the moral support, and the strategic answers to help you create your inspirational, best-selling book and get it out into the world in a big way, bringing you more authority, more influence, and more impact.

Dave Thompson
Founder of Inspirational Book Writers

Introduction
Where It All Began

"For anyone looking to achieve their lifelong dream to write a book and to tell your story, I highly recommend Inspirational Book Writers to bring your creation to life"
—Michele Jones, founder of Live Your Best Life.

Dave Thompson

This is the story of how Inspirational Book Writers came to be ...

It was January of 2014 in Melbourne. I'd been in my own business, coaching for about two years, having left my career as a lawyer back in 2011. I'd built up my client base, and had one-on-one clients who were getting great results.

I was looking around, asking myself "What's the next step? The next level? What will help me grow and expand in the coaching industry?"

It was suggested to me that I write a book.

The idea immediately resonated with me and rang true. I started looking around for ways to write the book. Some people I knew had done voice notes, then had that transcribed from, so I decided to try that. One afternoon I dictated about 15,000 words but to be honest, it was a mess.

Dictating the audio really didn't work for me because my ideas came out all jumbled and when I received the transcription back it required SO MUCH EDITING that it defeated the purpose. I felt deflated.

I started looking for other methods, when I came across the Tim Ferris book, *The 4-Hour Work Week*. He talks about Parkinson's Law and the Pareto Principle—that the task will grow or shrink depending on the time and space allocated for it, and that 80% of outcomes come from 20% of inputs.

So, I thought to myself,

"What if I gave myself a week to write this book?"

I was busy…running my business, coaching clients, and I really didn't have three or six months to sit in a hut in Bali and write my memoirs (though I was massively tempted).

I could, however, spare a week. I decided I would give myself Monday to Friday, and I would eliminate all distractions. My schedule was to go walking in the Melbourne Botanical Gardens from 8:00 a.m. to 4:00 p.m. I took no money, no food, no phone … so I could purely focus on writing. I also knew that the natural environment would work well for me as, like most people, I write better in nature.

Every morning I woke up, took out my notebook, started walking in the gardens, and when inspiration struck, I would write. I'd then get up, keep walking and repeat. To my surprise, it was finished by Thursday! (The surf at Torquay Beach was forecast to be PUMPING on Friday—so I got it done fast.)

I also didn't want to take forever to get it published. I'd just created this thing; I was excited and wanted to keep the momentum going! I looked into the industry and the only options I could find were a 6, 12, or 18-month turnaround. I'm a fast-moving, innovative entrepreneur … "there had to be another solution," I thought. I decided I would get it done as fast as I could at the highest quality possible. The other thing I knew was that if I waited too long, I would procrastinate, and the idea might die.

I had no idea where to start. I turned to one of my friends who said to me, "Dave—you just need to ask yourself the question, what do I need next?" This proved to be the foundation question for me to build the publishing process without getting overwhelmed.

As I soon discovered, book publishing has hundreds of small, tiny details, none of which are particularly difficult, but all of which must be completed in the right sequence. I don't know whether I am a sucker for details or that something higher was creating this process, but I set about learning all the micro-details about how to publish a book. I have an obsessive personality and soon enough I knew everything about how to publish a quality book. There were certainly some headaches down in the depths of learning the details though!

Once I understood the process, my interest was finding quality people to help me. I didn't want my book to look like a crappy throw-together, I wanted something that was professional and of a quality standard that could proudly sit alongside the best in the business.

This is where the idea for IBW began to emerge.

When I launched my first book in early March of 2014, I only expected to sell a few copies. I ordered 10 books and thought, "I'll be doing good if I sell 10 books!"

Within 60 days I'd sold 500 copies! I was blown away. I had readers in eight countries; people were posting on their Facebook about the book and taking photos with it, recommending it to their friends! People were placing bulk orders for their workplaces—10, 25, even 100 copies for one organisation! I could see and feel my profile being uplifted. In the two months following, I started getting an influx of enquiries, even more clients, clients who wanted to pay upfront and get started right away. Profile up! Income up! Visibility UP!

Photo: My First Book, March 2014

To be honest, I would have been really happy with that...I had no concept of what was about to be unleashed from one very special conversation—the birth of IBW.

A very close friend of mine, Michele Jones, who is a leadership coach in Australia and Asia, called me up and said,

> **"Dave, I've been wanting to write my book for seven years and you are telling me you wrote this in less than a week and had it published six weeks later???**
>
> **I WANT YOU TO TEACH ME THAT."**

In that moment I realised people had a need, a problem, a difficulty, and I had created a very unique way to solve that problem.

I had been wanting to take people away on retreat for 12 months, but I didn't know what we would do when we got there.

In that moment, time stood still, and it all became clear …

We are going on retreat to write books.

Someone pass me a coconut!

From 2014 – 2019, we ran twenty, week-long Inspirational Book Writers Retreats. It was an absolute blast, taking people to paradise, helping them write important, meaningful books. Everyone loved it, and in March of 2019, we led a group in our first overseas book retreat, held on the Big Island of Hawaii.

We had entrepreneurs fly in from all corners of the globe, and indeed, this retreat proved to be the birthing place for many international best sellers.

But, like with most things in life, times changed. After spending most of 2019 trying to figure out how to expand the business to be able to serve more people, I had the lightning bolt moment of inspiration coming back from the beach, one day in late November 2019.

I was speaking to a colleague who I had done a workshop with in 2014. Right after that call, I got the download for the Online Book Writing Intensive! The Intensive is the same retreat we would do on the island, just delivered virtually, and at a fraction of the cost.

Dave Thompson

We launched the first Online Book Writing Intensive on December 4, 2019, a full three to four months before the world went into lockdown over the coronavirus, when every coach on planet earth was forced to pivot online. I'm grateful that we were ahead of the curve.

At the time of writing, we don't know if we will ever be able to run events on the island again. Of course we trust and hope that we can get back to the island one day. Even if we can't, rest assured that the island spirit is infused in every single thing we do.

This book has been designed to give you the complete download on everything we have learnt about producing high-quality, best-selling books over the last six years.

So let's get into it!

Chapter 1
Before You Begin

State of the Union: Publishing—From Then to Now

Books have stood the test of time as humanity's greatest way of sharing wisdom, ideas, and stories. All the great religions of the world have a book that codifies their ideas.

The book, as we know it today, is over 500 years old with German man Johann Gutenberg acknowledged as the first human to print a modern-day book as we know it (the Bible, in Latin!). For most of this 500 years, writing, publishing, and launching a book was the domain of only the ultra-rich, ultra-educated, and ultra-connected.

Literacy and the ability to write were skills only a few had, and even if you could write, you would need permission from gatekeepers to publish your work. For example, famous Irish writer Oscar Wilde would not have had his work published had it not been for the connections of his parents.

(Side note: Oscar Wilde actually attended the 400-year-old Portora Royal School in Enniskillen, Northern Ireland—which was the school that signed me as a rugby coach in 2008 when I left university!)

Even in modern history, as recent as the early 2000s, there were still gatekeepers that could say YAY or NAY to your work being published. These gatekeepers were what we know as the traditional publishers—the big, behemoth publishers that will only say yes to printing your book if it will make them money. If you don't have a platform, or a sufficiently big platform to satisfy them, you won't get a look-in.

This old model of publishing left many highly talented people high and dry with their ideas, with nowhere to go. This old model also relied primarily on making money through book royalties (of which the publisher would keep 80 – 90% of those royalties!).

Thankfully, with the advent of the internet, new ways to get your ideas out into the world emerged. Those traditional publishers started to lose their grip on the gate! And what's more, a new, more innovative model of publishing began to emerge.

In the modern era, publishing is now not primarily about making money from royalties. Sure, you'll make a bit (our biggest book writer has done $120,000 in book sales), with most making enough for a nice holiday, but the real return on investment is from what comes AFTER the book.

The book is no longer the ends—it is now the means to the ends. Your inspirational best-selling book is the GATEWAY, it's the GOLDEN HANDSHAKE that opens the doors to wherever you want to go. That's one of the things I love most about books, is that they can be used to further so many goals.

- Want more speaking gigs, at a higher rate, in front of bigger audiences? A book will take you there.

- Want to sell high-ticket coaching and consulting? The credibility of your book will get you there.

- Want publicity and exposure to amplify your star power and impact on the world? A book will take you there.

And I could go on. The best thing about the new model of publishing is that you don't need a platform to get started, because you can use your book to BUILD a platform! Your book is the foundation piece from which to build everything else, because it gives you the credibility and authority, so people pay attention to your message.

There is power in your message that when unearthed can bring you Influence, Authority, and Impact and accelerate your personal and business evolution.

HERE IS YOUR OPPORTUNITY!

The 11 Prime Directives of Book Writing

Team sport, and in particular rugby union, was a huge part of my life. I played rugby for 14 years, and over that time there was one coach, Lachlan Ferguson, who had the biggest impact on my life. He was a towering man, with fists the size of a Christmas ham, and a powerful aura to boot. His mere presence commanded respect, let alone his impressive playing and coaching record. Every training session, Lachlan would drill us on an aspect of our game. He had many "sayings" or "Lachlan-isms" that he was known for.

One season in under 19s, we came off the field at half time having played significantly less than our best. We were expecting a rocket from our esteemed coach. Instead, he said to us,

> *"Gentlemen. That was rubbish and you know it. I say the same 20 things to you* EVERY SINGLE TRAINING SESSION. *There are only ever 20 things that can go wrong in a game of rugby. I've given you the best of what I've got, now you go and figure out what needs to change so you can win this game of rugby."*

And with that—he walked off and left us to it. That moment was forever etched into my being. Because it's so true, isn't it? When it comes to life, usually there is only a small number of things, of "Prime Directives," as I call them, that if you have sorted, will lead you to the promised land.

Now, over a decade later, I've coached enough book writers to know the "Prime Directives" for book writing success. So, before we go any further, here they are:

#1 Progress Over Perfection
You will never finish your book if you write one sentence, then go back and edit that sentence. That is the ultimate in perfectionism, and is a sure-fire way to make your book take 1000 years to complete. The attitude to adopt is one of progress over perfection.

#2 Go for the Low-Hanging Fruit
Some people like to make it hard for themselves. Don't be one of those people. In your book writing journey, I invite you to consistently keep taking action on the low-hanging fruit. Doing the easiest thing first builds confidence and momentum because you're then like, "Oh yeah! I just did something that moved this forward, WOO!"

#3 Just Take the Next Step
Ultra-marathon man Dean Karnazes famously writes about a 100-mile race he was competing in. It was in the desert, and he got to 80 miles and passed out, rolling off the side of the road, landing with a cactus in his back. When he regained consciousness, he realised he still had a gruelling 20 miles to go! But that was not the goal he set himself.

Instead, he set himself the goal of just rolling away from the cactus. "If I can just get away from this cactus, I'll be happy!" After minutes of trying, he managed to roll away from the cactus. His next goal was to stand up. He tried but fell down again, and rolled back into the cactus! Back to square one.

This to and fro with the cactus, and standing up, went on for about half an hour. Finally, he was able to stand. Then his goal became "just take one step." So he did, but then fell over and rolled back into the cactus!

He said he did not get frustrated, despite the one-step-forward-three-steps-back reality that had been playing out. He said that he knew if he could just persist with his "just take one step" approach, that eventually something would shift, and everything would click into place.

Finally, after two hours of up and down, he was able to take steps forward, walking, which then turned into slow jogging, which turned into running, and thanks to his persistence and "just take one step" approach, he was able to finish the race.

The same applies to book writing. Sometimes you will feel like you're in a cactus.

Remember this story in those times.

#4 Simplify

Overwhelm is one of the biggest challenges to a book writing journey. With so many unknowns, you can become saturated in uncertainty. So, it's super important to simplify.

Let me tell you a story. In early 2014, when I went to write my first book, there was only one other person I knew who had written a book—my friend Matt Kelly. I asked Matt how he did it. The simplicity of his approach has stuck with me all these years later. The conversation went like this:

Dave: "So, Matt, how did you write your book?"

Matt: "Well, I asked myself, what's the first thing I need for a book? The obvious answer is "words." So, I went and wrote words. Once I'd written words, I asked myself what I needed next. And the answer was editing. So, I went and found editing."

If you're ever stuck, it's probably because you need to simplify. Ask yourself what you need next, and then JUST GO DO THAT.

#4 Lean In

A sure-fire way to NOT write your book is to go into hiding. When you avoid facing what you need to face, you are letting the resistance win. If you acknowledge that the book writing journey can be a bit "sticky," then you can commit to "lean in" when the going gets tough.

LEAN IN—LEAN IN—LEAN IN—and then LEAN IN some more!

#5 Ask for Help
You are not on a deserted island. You are not a lone wolf. When writing your book, please ask for help. We have a rule that if you are stuck for more than 90 seconds, ask for help. There is no point wasting time stewing and lopping and going round in circles. Get the direction you need and keep going!

#6 Do What Works
We each have individual things that work for us. For example, some people are morning people, some work better in the evening. Some work better standing up, some work better sitting down. Some of our most productive book writers work best between 2:00 a.m. and 9:00 a.m.!

We even had one man, an entrepreneur and sales executive from Sydney, write his book on his iPhone because that's where he was most productive! He did not own a laptop and so wasn't familiar with typing, but on a daily basis he would write speeches on his phone to give to his organisation. In every instance, do what works for you!

#7 Action Creates Alignment
Many people sit back and wait for the perfect moment for the "stars to align" or for the moment when they finally feel "in alignment" to write their book. In every single instance, I have seen that taking action actually CREATES the alignment they are seeking.

Don't use "alignment" as an excuse—it comes through the action.

#8 Quit the Comparison
Flick on social media for even three seconds these days and you will see every man and his dog out there promoting their wares. Without a discerning mind, it can be easy to fall into the comparison trap of "ohhh, look what they are doing, they are way ahead of me!"

Fuck that.

This is your journey, and that's all that matters. Look to others for inspiration, but realise, you are not them, and they are not you. You've decided to do this book for your own deeply important personal and professional reasons. Stay focused on that, because that's all that counts.

#9 Dump It Then Refine It
Perfectionists find this idea so liberating! When you set out to write, it does not need to be perfect. Spew it out. Dump it out. Just get the words OUT! Don't judge what you are writing, just let it come!

When you dump out the words, oftentimes you'll find that it's missing something, there are spelling mistakes, or something isn't in there. Even in writing this paragraph, I can see two punctuation errors in my writing, but I'm not stopping, because I know that will be addressed in the refinement phase.

And don't worry if it's not quite the voice you want either—this can be addressed at the refinement phase. We once had a client write a book about health, and as she held multiple scientific degrees, her first dump of the book was quite dry, structured, and scientific. She then went on in the refinement phase to add in more emotion and make the words "feel" better to read.

#10 Get to 65% Complete as Fast as Possible
The unspoken fear of every first-time author is, "Can I actually do this?" And if you haven't written a book before, let alone a book in a week, I can understand your point. The antidote to this is to get to 65% complete as fast as possible. Because at 65% complete, your work becomes tangible, it becomes visceral, it becomes real! And that is inspiring and motivating, which is exactly the energy you need to propel you forward into the home stretch.

#11 Start-Maintain-Finish Or Start-Start-Start
One big idea that we focus on in the book writing week is START MAINTAIN FINISH. The first part of the week has an energy of START. It's the time to use your excitement to build momentum, get those first words down. MAINTAIN is the middle of the week, and it's all about adopting a steady energy of one foot in front of the

other, just keep moving, keep putting those words down. During the MAINTAIN phase, you will cross the halfway point. FINISH is when you bring it home! There is excitement at the prospect of finishing your book, and this is energising—keep going, you're almost there!

Another idea that has worked well for our book writers is the idea of START START START. This works particularly well for writers who are creators at heart. They love the crazy chaos of starting something, so often we will say to a creator, "Go start Chapter 1, now start Chapter 2, now start Chapter 3, now start your review, now start your final review," and so on. Using the language of STARTING is a useful hack to keep things fresh and engaging.

The Six Decisions of Book Writing

Before you begin the process of actually creating your book, there are some decisions to make. If you don't make these decisions, things get wishy-washy, and your book writing journey will be long, probably very painful, and drawn out. When you make the following decisions, things flow. I'm talking about making a legitimate, strong, committed decision here.

#1 The Decision to Speak Up
The decision to write a book is literally that—a decision. I'd known for two to three months that this book was on the way, and then on 15 February, 2020, I pulled the trigger and made a decision to write it. The decision to speak up, express, and share your message with the world is always a decision. I trust that if you haven't made that decision yet, that this book will give you the friendly kick up the ass to make that decision and get moving!

#2 Deciding to BE the Person That Writes Books
How do you get anywhere? You just go there. In 2011, my friend Matt Kelly decided he wanted to be a runner. That afternoon he bought some running shorts, and that night he went for a 10 km run. He is now a runner. The same goes with books, and being a writer.

Decide that you are a writer. Then be the writer, and write!

#3 The Decision to Be the Relatable Hero
Listen, the guru model is old and dying, just like the traditional publishing model. People these days want to learn from people they can relate to, not the gurus of yesteryear, who are essentially "untouchable."

Nowhere is this more evident than with Glenn Munso, best-selling author of *Drugs Do Not Discriminate*. Glenn had his own battle with drugs, and was able to successfully get off drugs through health and fitness. He now teaches his own five-step method to youth all over the country, and his book has sold over 4000 copies. He gets results because people can relate to him, because he is real, and not hiding behind academia.

#4 The Decision to Be Quirky AS FUCK!
Back when I was a lawyer, it was standard office practice to "check" your personality at the door every morning. Beige conformity was encouraged, and unique individuality was not permitted.

Oh, how times have changed! Your book will have the most success when you fully express your quirky and weird nature!

Are you weird? Welcome to the club! People want weird, unique, quirky. It's different.

It's new. It's art. It's attractive to your tribe.

Your uniqueness. Your voice. Your quirks. Your tribe. Your language.

This is what we need from you, in your book!

And just in case you needed permission to be weird (which you don't), here are 10 weird and quirky things about me:

1. When I was a baby growing up on a remote island in Papua New Guinea, instead of changing my nappy, my dad would hose me down with a garden hose. It was the tropics—it was warm—and it worked ;)
2. As a 10-year-old, I wore my pants WAY too high.
3. I had a man-crush on the band Hanson since the very beginning in the 90s.
4. In my 20s, I spent a ski season in Canada and every time there was a powder day, I'd ski down the hill yelling "POW, POW, POW!" at every turn.

5. I have an unusually strong passion for dragon fruit—they are like a totem of mine.
6. If I was a tree, I'd be a coconut palm.
7. I am obsessed with coconuts and coconut-related products.
8. I think astrology is a super practical way to predict the future.
9. I was Fletcher Christian from Mutiny on the Bounty in a past life.
10. I once met a 22-year-old Chinese girl in Sydney who made $5,000 per month selling frog fridge magnets on eBay.

So—let your freak flag fly!

#5 The Decision to Say It in Your Voice

I know many people who hold off writing their book because they "think" they need to write it in "proper" English. They think they are not good enough writers because they failed high school English. In the old-school publishing world, those beliefs were valid because the traditional publishing gatekeepers demanded that things be their way, for example, "proper."

Not anymore.

I don't give a fuck if you start your sentences with And. And I don't care if you want to use "wanna" slang, or make up brand-new words—your book is your expression, and your piece of art.

Another thing—writing your book in SIMPLE language is often best! It is often the most compelling way to get a message across. Love him or hate him, I have to admire the simplicity of the communication of the current US president, Donald Trump. He uses super, super simple sentences—but everyone understands him.

And another hot tip—if you are good at conversation, write your book in a conversational tone! Pretend that you are sitting down with your friends for morning tea. Pretend that you are having a chat, teaching them, showing them, informing them of what you've got to say. And then go write your book in that tone and voice!

#6 The Decision to Be Bold and Courageous in Leadership

It's hard to kind-of-half-maybe write a book. It really requires commitment—perhaps a greater level of commitment than you have shown to a task than ever before. That level of steely determination to do whatever it takes, until it takes, is what is required to see you through the writing, publishing, and launch stages.

And if you've really been listening to the nudges of your soul, it's probably been telling you that you have needed to write your book for a while now. Some of our clients have waited 15 years to write their book, and started to suffer health challenges because they were holding in their expression.

So, before you proceed and cause yourself unnecessary suffering by being half in, just decide right now that you are going to show up as a bold and courageous leader in sharing the message of your book.

It's taking your place on the stage, rising up and saying,

"WORLD, THIS IS WHAT I'VE GOT FOR YOU!"

Be the lighthouse for others.

Be the living, breathing, embodied example of what is possible.

Let's get started.

The Book Map is your first starting point.

Chapter 2
Getting Started With Purpose and Direction

The Book Map

"The Book Map is the best, most effective way to get started with your book, and save yourself months and potentially years of false starts, by starting out on the right foot!"—
Dave Thompson.

The Book Map is the first step in getting started on your inspirational, best-selling book. The first step is the biggest hurdle for most people. I've seen so many rush into their book, full of enthusiasm, only to find out later that the 5,000 or 10,000 words they have just written don't really fit in with the vision for the book. Enthusiasm to start is a great thing, but it is an energy that needs to be directed in a strategic way.

What you really need when you get started is DIRECTION.

That is exactly what the Book Map session provides. In this book, for the first time, I am going to reveal to you the exact process we use for all our high-end clients. The Book Map is strategic, intuitive, soulful, and practical. It helps you get clarity on your direction at all levels.

Sport was a big part of my life. I played rugby union for 12 years, and at the age of 26, played for Australia in Beach Handball AND ran a 100 km ultra-marathon in under 20 hours, all in the same year. In my time as an elite athlete, the quality of my warm-up often strongly influenced the quality of my performance. The same philosophy applies to book writing.

Before we even begin the planning in the Book Map session, we want to "warm up" and get in a great state.

The Warm-Up

Imagine you are going on the book writing journey. There are several qualities, characteristics, or you could say emotional states of being that will be important. Warming up is about switching on, activating the inner resources so you can make the best plan possible. The Warm-Up is designed to do exactly that.

So let's go!

The Warm-Up is a game of word association. I'll throw a word at you, and you just rattle off the very first things that come to mind:

INSPIRATION

_____

_____

_____

CREATIVITY

_____

_____

_____

PRODUCTIVITY

_____

_____

_____

*A note on these words. If a word has a negative connotation to it for you—switch the word for something that has a positive connotation!

Are you warmed up?! Great!

Let's get into the Book Map.

The Book Map Game Plan

The Book Map process has eight levels. We start big picture, with your purpose for the book, and at each level, we gradually become more and more specific. This is the best way to plan a book because if you think about it—what is a book? It is an idea, or set of ideas that have been out and about in the universe, just waiting for someone to bring those ideas into physical form (for example, a book).

Famous writer, Elizabeth Gilbert, in her book *Big Magic*, speaks of this process whereby creative ideas are just floating out there, waiting to latch onto someone who is willing to do the work to actually bring the idea to life.

So, we start big picture, connecting into your higher self (level 8)—the part of you that just KNOWS what needs to happen.

Then we get clear on your purpose (level 7) for the book—for both yourself in your life and business, and for others—the people reading your book.

Then we get even more specific, clarifying the vision (level 6) for your book—how does it look out in the world? What is it doing? How is it being used for impact?

Then we drop into level 5, which is the expression of the book. Here we create the title, sub-title, clarify the target audience, AND get clear on the tone/voice that will best express your message.

Next we get even more specific, dropping into level 4 (structure) and creating your chapter outline.

At this point, most book writing coaches would have you stop your planning. "You've done enough! Just get started now!" However, in my experience, if you actually get clear on levels 3, 2 and 1 (which I'll tell you about in a moment), then you can have an even more graceful and easy journey with your book.

Level 3 is about getting clear on your new identity. Writing a book and publishing means you become an "author" and if you work with us, an Amazon best-selling author (and perhaps even international best-selling author). But what else is happening as you up-level and accelerate your evolution? This is worth examining because it is POWERFUL. More on this below.

Level 2 is also often forgotten—it's about connecting in with a team to help you bring the book to life.

Level 1 is all about action—what are the next three steps to take?

Let's go into the Book Map process in detail. The best way to demonstrate this process is to actually share with you the Book Map that I created for this book!

Book Map Level 8—Connect to Higher Self
Take a moment to be still, and take a big deep breath.

What you are about to create is the plan for a book that will fundamentally accelerate your personal and business evolution. The ride is going to be EPIC, so take a moment to take it all in.

We start the Book Map session by connecting with your higher self—the part of you that just KNOWS which way to go and what to do. It is probably the part of you that guided you to be here, reading this book.

So, take that big deep breath in.

What does your higher self want you to know about the book you are about to plan and then write?

When I ask myself that question, my higher self answers:

> *This is a brand-new foundation for the business. It represents who and what Inspirational Book Writers is NOW, and it's a statement piece, containing your best work. Give this book everything you've got, give it your best, because this book is destined to be the best you've ever written. And another thing—be generous and proud of presenting this book to the*

world, as it will help so many people to unearth the power of their message, and accelerate their personal and business evolution.

WOW. How about that for powerful?

So, take a deep breath, and ask your higher self, what message does it have for you, about your book?

Write the answer below:

_____

_____

Book Map Level 7—The Purpose of Your Book
When we think about purpose, we look at it from two perspectives: what's the purpose for you, and what is the purpose for others?

Ultimately, what I think a book is about is getting your ideas out to the world in a bigger and better way, up-levelling your authority, influence, and impact in the world.

We can look at that from two perspectives: personally and professionally. If you're reading this book, there's a part of you that KNOWS that writing, publishing, and launching your book is the absolute KEY to unearthing the next stage of your evolution, personally and professionally.

From a professional/business perspective—an inspirational, best-selling book is a powerful vehicle for positioning, authority, and credibility.

"1000 copies in the first 48 hours and my practitioner training program sold out six months in advance. There's no question that publishing well-positioned books is REALLY good for business"—Dane Tomas, #1 Amazon Best-Selling Author of *Clear Your Shit*, and Founder of The Spiral Institute

For Dane Tomas, publishing *Clear Your Shit* in early 2016 was a power move as it codified his modality. There was now a tangible "book" to learn his transformational tools.

Here are 12 of the most common reasons why leaders write their book.

#1 Accelerate Your Authority and Credibility

All things equal, if a customer has the choice between two service providers, and one has an inspirational best-selling book, and the other doesn't, who are they more likely to go with?

If you said the service provider with the book, you're right. You become the person that literally "wrote the book" on your topic.

The fact is that people want to do business with people that they know, like, and trust. With a book, you get the opportunity to develop a level of intimacy with your audience that is not possible in traditional marketing.

It's like giving your reader your book and saying, "Here, take this; if you love the vibe and the message and the ideas in this book, get in touch, because we'd be a great fit to work together."

#2 Unearth the Power of Your Message and Accelerate Your Evolution as a Leader

Initially I was going to write this section and talk about competition, and how if you don't claim your space as a leader now, you might miss out. But that is fear speaking. It's competition based. It's old paradigm.

What I actually truly believe, what is present, what is current right now in the new world, is that when you write an inspirational book, you automatically rise up as a leader. There is power in unearthing your message. It accelerates your evolution. Those things are inherent in the process. They just "happen."

You want to share your message more—write a book.

You want to get on stage and impact people—write a book.

You want to actually BE the leader you've always talked about being—write a book.

The process of writing your book causes you to become SUPER clear on your message.

With this clarity comes precise communication. With that precision comes the ability to cut through the noise in the marketplace.

Practically speaking, your book is the golden handshake, or the VIP ticket that opens the doors to wherever you want to go.

#3 Leverage Your Expertise Into a 1:Many Vehicle

If you've been doing 1:1 delivery for any amount of time, you probably find yourself saying the same things to the same types of people, over and over and over again. You are probably bored at the sound of your own voice!

A book containing the best of your ideas, the top 20 things you always say to clients, the most common stories you always tell—this type of book can really save you a lot of time.

Instead of saying the same thing, just tell the client "it's all in the book!" The mental freedom and peace of mind from knowing you have essentially replicated yourself is priceless.

This is actually one of the most common reasons cited by our clients when we ask them why they wrote their book! Our clients in the health sector—chiropractors, kinesiologists, doulas, therapists of all types—are the ones who most commonly cite this reason for writing their book, though it equally applies to any 1:1 practice.

#4 Accelerate Your Speaking

Books and speaking are the ultimate pair. They go hand in hand and accelerate each other. If you have a book and start speaking, you will sell more books and programs, and if you're already speaking, your book will help you get on more and bigger stages. In fact, some events now will ONLY take speakers who have written a book—it is becoming a prerequisite.

You might want to go on a nationwide book tour, like Glenn Munso did. He helps youth get off drugs through health and fitness, and in 2017, took his book *Drugs Do Not Discriminate* on tour for 15 months to almost every state in Australia, selling 4000 copies in the process.

#5 Generate Media and Publicity

Traditional media like newspapers, magazines, and TV need experts for the various reports, news items, and segments they produce. Some websites like SourceBottle.com and HARO.com are dedicated to linking experts with media.

Jacqui Grant launched her book with us in December 2018 and by the end of January she was on the front cover of *Woman's Day* magazine with a double-page spread.

Relationship Coach EJ Love was featured in the same *Woman's Day* magazine before she had even commenced the publishing phase!

But the possibilities are not just in traditional media.

Ask Samantha Riley, who in 2015 launched *The Heart of Entrepreneurship*. She went on a "podcast tour," appearing on about 30 different podcasts, many of them with strong audiences in the United States. She was able to break into the US market, and now she does a significant amount of business in that market.

To watch case studies of our success stories, go to www.inspirationalbookwriters.com and click Case Studies.

#6 Build Out the Low-End of Your Funnel

When I started in business in 2011 as a personal coach, all I had to offer was my 1:1 premium coaching sessions. I had no way for people to try me out, get to know me or my work, or the transformation that I could create in their business and lives.

Sure, I could impress people in person and on sales calls, but there was nothing low-end in my business to help build the rapport with my clients. I wanted to put my prices up, but I felt like I couldn't, because I didn't have the credibility.

In early 2014 when I launched my first book, within 60 days my results in my coaching business just took off. I went from just getting by on $33k a year, to $100k/year. I attribute this to the authority, credibility and visibility my book gave me in the marketplace.

People could understand my ideas and philosophies, AND the book gave me credibility to charge a premium rate. I went from $2000 coaching packages with people paying on payment plans over long periods to $5000 coaching packages paid upfront. It was revolutionary for me.

(And honestly, my first book wasn't even that good! I'm actually kind of embarrassed about it!)

#7 Build a Money-Making, Sell-Books-and-Get-Paid-To-Receive-Leads Book Funnel

For six years, Russel Brunson had tried to launch Click Funnels to the world. It failed every time—until he wrote a book about it, and launched it in a book funnel. Suddenly, it worked! And now, Click Funnels is a $100m company.

Switched on marketers know that a book funnel is a golden strategy when you get it right. The book is offered for free and the client pays shipping, with various upsells and downsells of information products worked into the funnel.

It is an advanced strategy and does require a level of sophistication in your business. However, if that is you, there is the potential for the end result to be you selling books, and getting paid to receive qualified leads.

#8 Sell High Ticket Offers
When Dane Tomas launched *Clear Your Shit*, he sold $100k worth of practitioner training programs in the two weeks that followed the launch. And this was six months in advance of the actual training!

When you have so many eyeballs on your book, it is inevitable that a percentage of those people will want MORE of what you've got. If your book positions the next step for people, then your book effectively becomes a sales tool. It helps you pre-qualify people before you even speak to them, because if they have read the book and still want to talk to you, they are much more likely to be a high-quality lead.

#9 Generate New Opportunities in Business
Writing a book is a BIG talking point. Mention it, and people get curious. They want to know what it's about, why you are doing it, how you are doing it—they will want to know everything.

Savvy marketers know that "conversation" is the prelude to "conversion." The entire process of writing, publishing, and launching a book is an opportunity to start a conversation with your ideal audience.

We have seen so many book writers receive incredible new opportunities because their book was a trigger for a conversation that then opened the door to new opportunities, like joint venture partnerships, collaborations, and more.

#10 Become a Best-Selling Author
There's something special about seeing your book at #1 on the Amazon charts, especially when it's ahead of books and authors that you have admired.

These best seller accolades from Amazon can then be used to open doors to media and publicity opportunities, and open doors where previously there was no door. Heidi Dening with her 2019 book *Her Middle Name is Courage* is a prime example of this. Heidi did the online launch, became a best seller in multiple categories, and then used those accolades to springboard herself into articles in the *Sydney Morning Herald*, and speaking opportunities at International Women's Day.

#11 Be a Force for Good (Philanthropy)
Nicole McLellan's mission is to get yoga into schools. But when she set out to write her first book, she had no idea what it would lead to—she just KNEW it had to be written. After donating the proceeds of her book sales to charity, an idea for a not-for-profit of her own dropped in.

Rather than homework, she created The Om Work Project—a not-for-profit organisation that provides yoga scholarships to young women who can then bring yoga into their communities. All her book royalties go into the project, and she is now living her dream making such a big impact on the world.

#12 Complete a Personal Journey of Transformation

When you write your book, you are completing a hero's journey, and returning home with the wisdom that allows you to take the next step in your life. We have had clients that write their book and then fall in love with the partner of their dreams, we have had clients accelerate their weight loss journey and lose over 100 kg by sharing their story, we have had clients start not-for-profit organisations based on their book. It's not always all about the money, though that is still important. Writing your book can be the vehicle that accelerates your personal evolution to becoming the person you've always wanted to be.

Book Map Level 6—What Is the Vision for Your Book?

Take a moment to visualise your book, already written, already published, in your hands—you can touch it, feel it, the idea for the book is now a tangible, physical, visceral, real-life THING.

When we drop into Level 6, Vision, what we are really asking is:

How do you see your book out in the world?

What is it doing?

Where is it?

How is it creating impact?

What's your evidence for success? How would you know that your book is doing what it's meant to be doing in the world?

List out everything you see—from the macro to the micro.

The macro-successes could be things like:

- Your book gets you on big stages to speak
- Your book opens doors to meet high-level people in your space

- Your book sparks a movement that changes a community, a culture, or the world
- Your book becomes a timeless book that people refer to for the next 20 years

Micro-successes could be things like:

- You receive an email from someone in a far-off, foreign country who found your book on Amazon and wants to thank you for the impact your book had on their life
- Someone stops you in your local café and goes, "Oh, you're [INSERT YOUR NAME]! I've read your book!"
- You receive a five-star review on Amazon from someone who loved your book
- The countless people who you will never speak to, and never meet, but nonetheless your book impacted their lives for the better

So visualise your book out in the world—how do you see it?

Book Map Level 5—Message

Level 5 is about dialling in the MESSAGE of your book. We focus on the four key aspects of the Message for your book: title, sub-title, target audience, and tone/voice.

Title

The title of a book can make or break a book's sales success. Get the title right, and you will have people magnetised to it, and sales will be a breeze. Get the title wrong, and your amazing work could be left floundering and unread. Sure, a great cover design can make up some ground, but you really want to get the title, sub-title, AND cover design all lined up.

Think about the title like a billboard that you'd see when you're driving along a highway. What's the first thing you notice when you see a billboard? Your eye is likely drawn to a picture or image, AND some words. The words are usually short in number—in the one-to-three word range. Sometimes you might use a phrase for a title, of five words approximately, but typically I prefer books with one-to-three word titles.

Keep in mind that there is ALWAYS exceptions to these general rules, so go with what FEELS best for you. In fact, we have had several clients over the years that have chosen titles and I've been like, "There is no way I would call it that!" But they loved the title so much, it resonated so much for them, that they ran with it, and had great success!

You want to go for words that are BIG and BOLD. Words that POP. Words that inspire curiosity. Words that speak directly to the reader's pain.

Here are some different types of titles that have really worked for our clients:

The Powerful Message Title
The powerful message title is the most common title format we use at Inspirational Book Writers. It involves using a short, powerful, punchy, memorable phrase as your title. Typically, these type of titles are one to five words in length, with the average being three words in length.

Examples:
Drugs Do Not Discriminate by Glenn Munso
Clear Your Shit by Dane Tomas
Become the One by EJ Love
Cut the Crap by Joanne Antoun

Identity Titles
An identity title is one that contains an identity that people aspire to being.

For example, in 2018, investment advisor Salena Kulkarni wrote the book *The Freedom Warrior: How to build a bigger life through alternative property investment strategies.* For people who identify with the warrior, and value freedom, this book speaks DIRECTLY to them.

Likewise with leadership coach Stacey Ashley's first book, *The New Leader.* For people who have been thrust into a leadership position for the first time, this book speaks directly to them.

Examples:
The Freedom Warrior by Salena Kulkarni
The New Leader by Stacey Ashley
The Mumfit Book by Alison Simpson

The "Tell Them Exactly What They Are Getting" Title
I once heard Taki Moore say that the best way to explain your message is to give them the "snakes on a plane" version. Whatever does he mean?! Well, if someone tells you there were snakes on a plane, it is quite obvious—there was a plane, there were snakes, and the snakes were on the plane. It is very meat and potatoes. There is meat (vegan meat, if you're vegan) and potatoes. It is SUPER clear what you are getting.

Normally we encourage our book writers to be super clear like this in the sub-title. But sometimes it works in the title instead.

Here are some examples:
Vendor Management by Agostino Carrideo
The Art of Powerful Communication by Maria Pellicano
Empowered Pregnancy by Sara Winchester

Sub-Title
Sub-titles are often forgotten and rarely done well. They seem to be an afterthought and not very well understood, so allow me to share some perspective.

A sub-title LANDS the book. It also should work in tandem with the title, that's why often you will hear me say, let's talk about your title and sub-title combination. If the title is the BIG BOLD statement to the world that attracts attention like a billboard would on the side of a highway, then the sub-title is what grounds the book, makes it real, makes it practical, makes it tangible so readers can actually understand WHAT your book is about.

The sub-title is best when it gives greater context and substance to the title. A sub-title will often answer these questions:

- Tangibly, what is the reader actually getting in the book? A guide, a set of tools, a methodology, story-telling, keys, principles, lessons, insights—pick a word that best describes what they get.

- Who is the book for? Is it for ambitious leaders, six-figure fitness pros, busy mums, etc.?

- What results do they get from the book? This could be tangible things like money or intangible things like confidence.

- Add in sparkle words (for example, adverbs) to bring the title to life. For example, Sara Winchester added the word "secret" into her sub-title "The *Secret* Wisdom of Natural Birth."

In terms of length, there really is no limit to how long or short a sub-title can be. We quite like long sub-titles because they allow room for you to pack in keywords, which is excellent for Search Engine Optimisation (SEO).

Here are some different types of sub-titles.

The A-B-C Sub-Title

Tim Ferris popularised this type of sub-title with his first book *The 4-Hour Work Week* (still one of my all-time favourite books and a HUGE influence on my journey and getting started back in 2008). The sub-title for that book was *"Escape 9 – 5, Live Anywhere and Join the New Rich"*—it's an A, B, and C sub-title.

The A-B-C sub-title gives the reader the three key takeaways, or results, that they will get from reading the book.

Leigh Rorke does this really well too. Her 2019 book *Soul Truth*, had an A-B-C sub-title of *"Get Unstuck, Live Your Truth, Awaken Your Power."*

Mia Munro used this format in her 2020 release of *The Human Reinvention Formula—"Escape Burnout, Create Sustainable Wealth, Join the New Breed of Superheroes."*

The A-B Sub-Title
The A-B sub-title is similar to the A-B-C, but it only includes two outcomes instead of three.

The How-To Sub-Title
The how-to sub-title is a really solid choice as a structure for a sub-title. It is sometimes not the most exciting format (as it has been used many, many times) but book writers continue to go back to it because it is so solid and reliable, and you can't really go wrong with it!

The essence of the how-to sub-title is it tells the reader how to do something, or how to solve a problem they have, or how to transform their situation from X to Y. If your book is about a transformational process, this structure fits really nicely.

Examples:
- *ON Track; How to lead research projects with clarity and confidence* by Dr Nadine Sinclair
- *RICH!; How to build an eight figure empire* by Karen O'Connor
- *Drugs Do Not Discriminate; How to overcome and recover from drug addiction* by Glenn Munso

Dr Nadine Sinclair wrote *ON TRACK* at the Hawaii book retreat on the Big Island in 2019. She helps PhD researchers keep their research projects ON TRACK (because their problem is getting stressed out and getting behind on their projects). She used a how-to sub-title that works REALLY effectively for her market.

The sub-title was: *"How to leader research projects with confidence and clarity."* Although this sub-title didn't explicitly name the transformation from

X to Y, it does this implicitly. If someone is looking for confidence and clarity, the pre-supposition of them picking up the book is that's what they want, because they either don't have it, or don't have enough of it.

Drugs Do Not Discriminate by Glenn Munso is another great example of a how-to sub-title. What I love about this sub-title—*"How to overcome and recover from drug addiction"*—is its simplicity.

It just tells you EXACTLY what you are getting in the book. Don't overcomplicate things; simplicity is often the best path.

The WHAT Sub-Title
I love this structure for sub-titles because of its simplicity. I want to emphasise simplicity again. Just like Sergei the Meerkat in that TV commercial (add link), keep things "SIMPLES."

This structure literally tells the reader WHAT they are getting.

Examples:

Dane Tomas with his famous 2016 text, *Clear Your Shit*. The sub-title for this is: *"A bible for accelerated evolution."* Super simple. You are getting a bible. The purpose of that is to help you accelerate your evolution. SIMPLE.

Sara Winchester in her 2017 title *Empowered Pregnancy*—the sub-title is *"The secret wisdom of natural birth."* SIMPLE. You are getting secret wisdom, pertaining to natural birth. Want that? If yes, BOOM! This is the book for you.

Keep it simple, folks, keep it simple.

Target Audience
Another consideration at level 5 is the target audience. Note that this is not about robotically doing an old-school analysis of the demographics and being like "oh, my target market is 25-35-year-old women who make over $100k per annum." There is nothing wrong

with demographic targeting like that and often it is a powerful way to market a book, especially if you are running targeted adds.

The approach that I find works best for our book writers is to focus on the characteristics that unite their readers.

- What is the pain that is common among your target audience? What do they frequently get frustrated about?

- What is common about the stage of the journey they are at? Are they in similar places on the journey, for example, just getting started, just waking up to possibility, just realising there is more to life, or more advanced—they are kicking butt but now it's time to go fully totally next level!

If you have multiple target markets, or two types of people (beginners and advanced, for example) that you work with, you can speak to both in your book. Nadine Sinclair did this exceptionally well in *ON TRACK*; check it out if you want to see how she pulled it all together.

Another great tip for ensuring your book speaks to your target market is by taking out your A4 notepad, and drawing a face of the person you are writing the book for. Place that picture in front of you when you are writing. You can even speak to your sketch and ask them what they want you to say in the book! I remember Ryan Parson doing this on the Hawaii book retreat in 2019; his person was Bob, from memory!

Keeping room for the unimaginable magic

A final word on target market. Unless you are a really sophisticated business owner and know EXACTLY who your ideal client is, I really encourage you to not be rigid in your application of this target market idea. Yes, it is great to have a clear idea of who you are writing for, but it is equally as valuable to be open to the magic. A prime case in point—Michele Jones wrote *Live Your Best Life* in 2015, aiming it at business leaders who wanted to live their best life. It sold strongly with that market—AND it also sold a stack of copies to young people, teenagers! And this is a 400-page book full of coaching tools! You can never be 100% sure who the book is going to land with, so be open to the magic of the possibility.

Tone/Voice
Pausing for a moment to consider the tone and voice of the expression of your words in the book is a great thing. How do you want your book to be expressed? What flavours do you want to come through?

Authentic
Raw
Real
Powerful
Fire
Authoritative
Loving
Caring
Flowing
Humorous

What voice do you want to write your book in?

Book Map Level 4—The Chapter Structure
When you nail a great structure, your book will feel good and make sense to the reader. It will be the perfect combination of logic and emotion, of masculine direction and feminine flow.

The structure of a book is made of three major parts:

#1 The Front Material
1. Title page
2. Copyright page
3. Dedication page
4. Table of contents page

#2 The Body of the Work
1. The introduction
2. The chapters
3. The conclusion

#3 The Back Material
1. About the author
2. Contact the author
3. Sales page/offer
4. Anything else relevant to your book (Resources List, References, Glossary, etc.)

The Introduction

You have about 10 seconds to capture the reader's attention at the top of the book. If you are boring from the get-go, it's unlikely the reader will give you a second chance. That's why it is SUPER important to be MEGA compelling in your introduction.

I think the easiest and most compelling way to start your book is by telling a story. Start with one line, or one sentence, that has an element of drama or emotion or fire or mastery or human connection to it.

For example:

He was done. Fuck that—this has to change—he couldn't put up with the XXX anymore!

The story can be just a paragraph in length, it doesn't have to be long—but it must be compelling.

Flowing on from that, there are actually eight key things that we have found that make a compelling introduction. We've noticed that if you put these eight things together (the order doesn't matter so much) then you will have set the scene for what is to come. And that's what you want to do in the introduction—set the scene.

Almost like people walking onto your front porch and you saying, "Welcome, welcome! So glad you're here. This book is for XX type of people, who are facing AA type of problems. I'll be sharing with you stories and techniques to help you solve that problem, and that is based off what I learnt in DD life situation. So, if you're up for the ride, join me now—who is in?!"

Notice how you are REALLY framing it up to the reader. You're forcing them to consciously or unconsciously say YES to joining you for the book, or making them opt-out if it's not for them.

If you'd like to download the Introduction Builder for FREE—go to www.inspirationalbookwriters.com/free

Chapter Outline—Putting Your Ideas Into Containers

Now that you've got the overview of the structure of the book (front material, body of work, and back material), and now that you know what to put in your introduction, it's time to create your chapter outline.

The first concept to understand is to think about your chapters like containers for your ideas. Consider this metaphor—have you ever done food prep? You know, where on Sunday afternoon you cook up a whole heap of food, ready for the week ahead. You might cook the chicken (or tofu), the broccoli, and the brown rice. Now, it makes sense to put those three foods in the same container. The foods are like your ideas. What ideas does it make sense to put together?

And here's the thing. There is no right or wrong with this—that's the beauty of it being YOUR book, you get to decide. Now, if you wanted to put some ice-cream in with the steamed broccoli, that's probably not going to make sense, unless your book is really eccentric and about revolutionary new, creative ideas. What I want to impress on you here is that you can put your ideas together in whatever way works for you.

The first step is to get the overview of the chapters, by listing them out. The next step is to go deeper into the structure of each chapter, which we will go into shortly.

Creating Your Chapters

The first question I ask every book writer at this stage of the Book Map is:

If you are going to best communicate your concept to the reader, what is the FIRST thing they need to know?

And you'd respond with, "Well, they'd need to know this, and this, and this."

List out the big chunks of ideas, until you can't think of anymore. Don't worry about getting them all out on the first pass, just get them down—remember, progress over perfection.

Now that you've got a brainstorm of the different sections, ask yourself, "Is there anything else that they need to know?"

What else?

Is there anything else?

Keep a list of random ideas, or ideas that you're not sure where they go, or whether they are ideas for this book or the next book.

Typically, our book writers will divide their ideas into anywhere from 5 – 12 chapters of anywhere from 1,000 – 5,000 words. Sometimes, those chapters will be grouped together into Parts; for example, Part 1 of the book has chapters 1 – 3, Part 2 of the book has chapters 4 – 6, etc. Again, separating your book into Parts is not compulsory, but can be useful if it makes sense for your teachings.

Chapter Structure

I said before that the Book Map process gets more and more specific the deeper you go. This is what happens with chapter structure. Read this section if you want some help on WHAT to actually write in each chapter.

I first came across the 4MAT model when doing my coach training in Melbourne in 2011. It was first created by Virginia Satir as a way to communicate with people of all different communication styles. Some people really want to know WHY the topic is important, others are more interested in WHAT you're actually talking about, some want to know the HOW, and others just want to race to the end and find out WHAT'S NEXT! So, if you write your chapters and answer each of these questions, you will be communicating with people in all different styles. We have a full video training and worksheet on this—if you'd like to get it for free, go to www.inspirationalbookwriters.com/free

If you're overwhelmed and feeling like your book is getting ENOURMOUS and potentially too big and unwieldly, then the chances are you have put in far too much of the HOW. This is not a good thing for you or the reader, especially if you are writing a book to position yourself as an authority in your space.

A really meaty HOW section can not only be a pain in your butt to write, but also a pain in the butt for the reader to consume. Barnes and Noble research shows that books of 80 – 100 pages get read from start to finish 80% of the time. Once the book gets bigger than that, people have to come back for a second, third, or fourth sitting to read the book (and sometimes they won't come back, because life gets in the way).

What you want is to give the reader a TASTE that leaves them desiring MORE. Let me explain by way of a story. Several years ago, I went to my cousin's wedding in Sydney. The venue was down by the water, and seafood was on the menu. A waiter came up to me with a plate of shot glasses—inside was the most DELICIOUS pan-seared scallop with lime that I have EVER eaten. It was mind-blowingly deliciously GOOD. Then he walked off—and for the rest of the night, I was chasing him down, trying to find MORE of this delicious scallop.

The moral of this story: be the scallop.

Give people a taste of WHY your topic is important and tell them WHAT they need to know. This should be enough of a taste to entice them to find out more, and that's when they enter a program, course, or other offering of yours, to get more of the HOW. And just to be abundantly clear—the HOW is often the implementation, and what they pay you for should they want to go deeper with your content.

Book Map Level 3—Become the Embodiment of Your Message

It was a sweaty, humid afternoon in late March. We were clambering our way up from the Pololu Valley, on the North Kohala Coast of the Big Island, Hawaii. We had just completed our first ever Hawaii book retreat, and this was our celebration/integration walk to round out the week. Our crew were taking little snippets of video, and when the camera turned to me, the gold came pouring out:

"Our process is different because you literally embody your message, you become your message, you own your message—and this all happens naturally in the process of writing it in such an intensive way."

Writing a book is a transformational process. You are literally ending one chapter of your life, capturing the wisdom in your book, and beginning a new chapter. It is the classic hero's journey playing out (Joseph Campbell). In that process, there is a death of the old self, and a birth of the new self. When you know that THIS is the process happening subconsciously, you can better navigate the journey. Most people think of writing a book as something you DO, not something you BE.

The BE-ING is SO important these days. Customers can smell a fraud from a mile away, and if you are out of integrity, it shows. I always remember Dane Tomas writing his first book, *The Conscious Hustle*, and coming to me in a break from writing saying he had some clearing to do to come into alignment with EVERYTHING he wanted to say. I think that's normal, and indeed the most responsible path. It will lead you to the most success.

If you are over-reaching, for example, trying to teach something that you have not done yourself yet, it shows. I remember one of our first book writers coming to me and saying they wanted to write a Paulo Cohello-esque fable-story-type book. They had never written before, and did not regularly practise their writing, and this was their first book. They tried for about an hour to write that book, and then realised they were over-reaching—trying to write something that was beyond the wisdom of where they were at the time.

The key takeaways are to:

#1 Be okay with where you are at, and write from that place.

#2 Understand that you are embodying your message on a whole new level, leaving behind an old identity and claiming a new identity in the process.

Practically speaking—what does this mean?

Firstly, every single person walks out of our program as an author. They are literally the person that "wrote the book" on that topic. There is expertise in that, and additional authority, credibility, and positioning.

The Hawaiians call it "mana"—in reference to the unseen, intangible energy that is conferred on people and places of importance. I believe that when you go through the process of writing, publishing, and launching a book, your mana is up-levelled. You become a person of note (or greater note), your self-esteem and confidence goes up, there's a shine to you that is attractive and magnetic to your ideal clients. You radiate with the leadership of someone who has taken the action to have their work published in the world.

This happens because you've stepped up. You're OUT THERE, proudly sharing your message. You're being seen for your talents and gifts. You're taking up space with your presence, your message, and your voice. You're shining the light. All of this, and more, happens when you write, publish, and launch your book.

Some examples of how this has played out for clients:

One client established the legitimacy of their healing modality by writing a book, codifying the modality. It is now registered with the International Institute of Complementary Therapies.

Another client used their book to shake up the way business is done in their industry. By presenting an alternative, disruptive set of ideas on how to do things, this client has established an identity in their industry as someone with something to say, and as someone who is prepared to speak out.

Another client used their book to go from social media famous to actual household name famous.

Some questions for you to consider at this identity level.

Who are you becoming through the process of the book?

What do you want to let go of?

Who do you want to step into being?

Book Map Level 2—Connection to Team

This is a vital step to consider in the Book Map. It really does take a team of people to put together a book, it's not just you, the creative voice, writing the words. Its editors, formatters, cover designers, printers, distributors—the list of people involved in even a single book project is quite extensive. Sure, you can organise all of this yourself, but it does take time and effort to find the right people for the job.

Our Publish + Launch service is designed to have everything you need to do exactly that—publish and launch your book. You can plug into the resources and system of our team to get your book done fast and at high quality.

Go to www.inspirationalbookwriters.com/publish-launch to find out more.

Questions to consider:

Who is going to support you in the book writing journey?

Who will help you with publishing and launching?

Book Map Level 1—Time to Take Action

This is the final step of the Book Map process. Now that everything is aligned, and you have clarity on all levels, it's time for the rubber to hit the road.

It's time to engage the "Matt Kelly" strategy of asking yourself, what is literally the one thing that will help you move forward right now?

What are the very next three things to help you move forward?

Chapter 3
Write Your Book in a Week

Quantum Book Writing Strategies

The very idea of writing a book in a week is a remarkable proposition. It is one that several people have questioned whether it is even possible. And I guess the question is fair enough—if you don't know the following strategies, then yeah, it's going to be hard to finish in a week! But on the other hand, when you GET how to flick into the Quantum flow state, you can instantly see, feel, hear, and KNOW it is more than possible.

> *"To write 22,000 words in a week and feel quite nourished is rather remarkable"*
> Dane Tomas

To give you an idea, we have had book writers finish a 35,000 word book in 30 hours—and eight of those hours were for sleeping!

We have had book writers produce 100,000 words in five days.

70,000 words in 3.5 days.

I myself wrote my last book of 22,000 words in 20 hours of writing time.

In this book I'm 25,000 words in and I've been going 22 hours.

Frequently, the "average" client will produce a 20,000 – 30,000 word book quite comfortably in five days of writing.

A reminder too that it's not always about size. We have published books with 4,000 words. As popular culture tells us, it's not how big it is, it's what you do with it!

Strategy #1—Activate Your Book Writing Container

Do you remember in high school when you would be given a big assignment that would be due at the end of the 13-week term? Typically, you'd leave it right to the last minute, right? Somehow, you'd pull it together in time.

That's because Parkinson's Law is in play. Parkinson's Law states that the size of a task will swell or shrink according to the amount of time allocated to it. Give yourself years to write your book, that's what it will take. Give yourself months, that's what it will take. Give yourself a week—that's what it will take.

Committing to a definitive START and FINISH time is very important for Parkinson's Law to work in your favour.

The other big advantage of setting aside the time for the book writing container is the focus, creativity, and momentum that can be built inside the container. People that write an hour a day all year often will struggle to build momentum. But when you set aside a week to write your book, you get to benefit from the momentum that you create. To give you perspective, what I've often seen is book writers who make a small amount of progress on days one and two—maybe 2,000 words each day—then by day three something clicks, the momentum swings in their favour, and BOOM! Their book is done inside 24 hours.

The other important aspect to a powerful book writing container is for it to be distraction free. Our clients frequently surprise themselves with their level of productivity when the distractions of social media and modern life are turned off.

Strategy #2—Activate the Pareto Principle (80/20 Rule)

The Pareto Principle states that 80% of the outcomes come from 20% of the inputs. Sometimes it swings even more extreme—99% of the results come from 1% of the actions.

I love this law for book writing because it compels you to focus on the mission critical tasks, like actually getting the words down on paper. It compels execution, brings in a get-it-done energy, and leads you to the outcome in the shortest time.

Practically, this means doing things like just dumping out the words, letting them flow out of you, without regard for spelling or grammar in the moment. It means not writing a paragraph, then rereading it, checking it, changing it, and reworking.

Let it flow! Let it flow! Let it flow!

This requires a deep sense of trust in self—trusting that what is flowing through you is in fact THE thing that needs to go down on paper. Perfectionists and overly logical people who overthink, or people who are worried about what others will think of their work may find this strategy confronting at first. But trust me (trust yourself really), it is THE way to get the book done in a week.

Strategy #3—Activate Flow State

A guy by the name of Mihaly Csikszentmihalyi wrote a great book titled *FLOW*. In that book, he talks about how flow is created. He says that flow is best created when the size of the task is not too hard, but not too easy either. If the size of the task is too much, too hard—the task will feel like a burden and the person will drop out of flow. Similarly, if the size of the task is too easy, or too small, the task will feel far too easy and it doesn't produce flow. Therefore, to summarise, Csikszentmihalyi is saying that what we need to engender a flow state is a task that is challenging, but within reach of our current levels of skills and abilities.

Writing a book in a week is definitely that. It is challenging, but totally possible, as over 130 book writers have shown over the last five years. Our book writers often say to me, "Wow! I believe it is possible, but GEE WHIZ, I'd have to show up at my best for that!" And that's the thing, writing a book in a week is a challenge, but if you show up with your best, it is totally possible.

Practically speaking, we break down the big challenge of writing a book in a week into a series of smaller writing assignments. If you want to write a 25,000-word book in a week, that's 5,000 words a day with two days spare for refinement and reviewing. If you do two writing sessions a day, that's 2,500 words per session.

Or put another way—if your book has 10 chapters, and you write them over five days (with two days for refinement and review) then you are writing two chapters per day, one in the morning, one in the afternoon.

Strategy #4—Collapse Time and Space Using Heart Space Zero

Whenever you enter one of our book writing containers, your sense of time will begin to shift. Our clients often remark that they feel like time has stood still for a week, or that they have been in a time warp all week. So much was achieved, but yet it felt like it happened in just a day or an hour!

Me and my team are trained in hypnosis so yes, there are a few magic tricks going on in the background to help you enter into a state of light trance, which basically leaves you feeling in your heart, pumped and excited, and with a different perception of time—namely that A LOT happens in a VERY short period of actual human recorded time.

The key to all of this is tapping into the heart space zero. The human heart, when fully activated, emits a frequency, a love vibration, you might call it, where manifestation of your heart's desires happens seemingly instantly! So, when you go to set up your environment to write, set it up so that your heart space is activated. That might mean your favourite food, your favourite view, your favourite rug, your favourite music—whatever gets you into your heart.

Strategy #5—First Class Care for Your Physical Body

At first glance it might be a bit odd that we are talking about physical body care in the Quantum section! Isn't this meant to be all supernatural, super-flow-type stuff, I hear you ask?! Yes. It is. And—we are still human. We have a human body. Thus, we must take care of it. Particularly when book writing, because think about it—in the

Quantum Reality your book is just an idea, a vibration, out there in the universe floating around, just waiting for some courageous human like you to go "YES! That's mine! I'll write a book on that!" And so begins the process of turning an idea into physical reality.

You are literally using your human body to birth this new thing (your book) into the world. Some have likened the book process to birthing a baby—however, I am cautious to wantonly go with that metaphor because sometimes birthing a human can be traumatic, and truth be told it is really unnecessary for the birth of your book to be that. In fact, your book can be one of great passion, excitement, and pride. Yes, sometimes there is fucking hard work involved, sometimes you really gotta roll up your motherfucking sleeves and get that shit DONE, but honestly, it doesn't have to be traumatic. So pick your metaphors wisely.

And look after your physical body while you are writing the book. This means great nutrition all week, keep your hydration up, exercise and stretch, particularly your shoulders and neck. Get great sleep, and always remember to breathe deeply.

It feels a little weird to be giving physical health advice in a book writing book, but honestly, the more you give to your physical body, the easier your journey will be.

Strategy #6—Your Power Move
You might be familiar with the New Zealand All Blacks Rugby Union team, and their haka. The haka is a tribal dance, done as a group, to inspire energy and passion within the group before heading into battle with the other team. The haka is the power move that lights up the NZ team, and in over 100 years over rugby, they have an 80% success ratio!

This is a testament to their power move/s.

In all of our week-long programs, we have our participants create their own power move. It is usually one move, and one sound, that inspires them and represents who they are, where they have come from. It might be a fist pump, a slap of the legs, more flowy and feminine—your power move can literally be anything that inspires power from within your soul.

Finally—Practicalities of Book Writing

I couldn't move on to the Publish section without discussing two of the most important practicalities for writing a book in a week—accountability and check-ins.

Let's be clear. Accountability does not mean "your book Sherpa writes your book for you." You still have to create the words, but accountability is important. Without accountability, books take YEARS to complete, if not they fall off the side of the earth and get lost in the dusty desk drawers of "ONE DAY."

Writing a book is WAY easier when you do it with a group of people on the same mission as you. Climbing Mount Everest solo is possible, but it's damn hard. The best accountability will champion you, buoy your spirits when the road ahead looks bleak, and keep you focused on your very next step. One question we ask on repeat in our book writing group is "What is THE NEXT step to help you move forward?"

The other part of accountability is the check-in process. Short, regular check-ins help to keep tabs on progress, keep the goals short, and easily achievable. As the saying goes, how do you eat an elephant? One bite at a time. (Unless you are vegan! In which case eat tofu. Side note: I once deeply offended a staunch vegan with that elephant joke!)

Chapter 4
Publish a High-Quality Book

Out With the Old
In With the New

Before the internet, it was really hard to get your work published. A select few held all the power, and would only grant access to publishing books they KNEW would make money for them. You needed prior success as an author, a celebrity profile, or a "BIG" name to even get a publishing deal.

Traditional publishing houses would rarely take a bet on new, upstart authors because it just did not make financial sense for them. They wanted to back the "sure thing," the "guaranteed winner."

An additional note here—even if you did get a deal with a traditional publisher, they would take almost all the royalties (you would get 10 – 15%), it would take 18 – 36 months for the book to be published, they would heavily edit and sensor what you could say, AND you would still largely be responsible for the marketing campaign behind the book.

It really was a case of you, the book writer, taking all the risk, doing all the work, and the traditional publisher getting all the rewards. But still, people loved having a brand name on the back of their book (like Hay House, for example) and so they would accept oppressive deals like this.

Then came the internet, and soon after, self-publishing was born. Self-publishing platforms started sprouting up everywhere and in the space of a decade, access to publishing became universal—if you had something to say, and an internet connection, you could publish your work to the world. Traditional publishers lost their position as gatekeepers to publishing. Self-publishing brought with it many benefits that were simply not present in the traditional publishing model.

Firstly, YOU, the book writer, keeps ALL the royalties (keep in mind the publishing platform does take a percentage for hosting your book, but there is no other gatekeeper taking a cut). You, the book writer, also retain 100% creative control over your work—you have the freedom to express your message the way you want to express it!

Also, it's fast to market. You can write something, have it edited, formatted, create a cover design, and BOOM! You can be published in hours or days, at most. There is also the flexibility to relatively easily make changes to your work, should you want to add in new material or do a revised/updated edition later on.

But while self-publishing platforms bring all of those benefits, there are some drawbacks. Self-publishing is accessible to everyone, and the barrier to entry is low. What this means is that sometimes self-publishing gets a bad rap in the press for presenting low-quality books. I understand that, because many people do go to websites like Fiverr and spend $5 on a cover design and then publish their work. It is just not that professional. Quality suffers.

When I wrote my first book in 2014, I started looking for publishing options. Looking around and seeing what was available in the traditional publishing and self-publishing spaces, I really wasn't happy with my choices. I didn't want to wait three years for my book to come out—I'm in business and time is money so I want my work out in the world working for me as fast as is practical! I didn't want some pokey editor slashing my work to shreds with their red editorial pen—I want to express my book and share my message the way I want to express my message! I didn't want to do all the work and then someone else get the majority of the rewards from my awesome-ness—I wanted to fully reap the rewards from the energy I put into the project. And finally, with self-publishing, I didn't want to create something cheap and nasty—I wanted something I could be proud of!

So that's why I created a hybrid publishing system, bringing together the best of traditional publishing and the best of self-publishing.

	Traditional Publishing	**Hybrid Publishing**	Self-Publishing
100% Creative Control	No	**YES**	Yes
100% Royalties	No	**YES**	Yes
High-Quality Book	Yes	**YES**	No
Fast to Market	No	**YES**	Yes
Accessible to First-Time Authors	Not always	**YES**	Yes

Our hybrid publishing system brings together the best of both worlds and delivers them to you. It is exactly what I wanted back in 2014 when I started, but it didn't exist back then, so I created it.

Modern Hybrid Publishing
Hybrid publishing is the perfect fit for the modern entrepreneur who wants to get their message out to the world in a BIG way. You get a high-quality book, produced in weeks not years, AND you keep 100% of the creative control, and royalties while maintaining your authentic voice. Here's how our modern hybrid publishing system works:

Read, Review, Give Me Feedback
Before the formal publishing process begins, you want to be sure your work is ready, and you haven't missed anything. Having experienced eyes review your manuscript can help you sharpen up the 1%ers and give you the confidence that you are putting your best work forward.

Editing
When it comes to editing, you want to get a quality copy edit completed on your work. A copy edit will tidy up all the spelling and grammar, sentence structures, tenses, highlight the parts that could be clearer.

Be aware of perfectionist tendencies at the editing stage, as often the perfectionist will fuss over a choice of words that really has negligible overall impact on the work.

You can find editors on freelance marketplaces like Upwork, with good editors starting from $40/hr.

Formatting

After editing and before you print your book, you will need to have it formatted for print and eBook. It is a specialised skill so find someone that has experience in book layout in both formats.

For print, your printer will usually require a print-ready PDF file set up according to their print template. We use the US Trade Paperback 6 x 9 inch trim size.

For eBook, ask your formatter for .EPUB and .MOBI file types. Most platforms will accept .EPUB; however, Amazon requires a .MOBI file.

Formatting cost depends on the size of the book and can be anywhere from $100 – $1500.

Cover Design—Front Cover

It really is true that people judge a book by its cover. It's the first impression for a reader, and it's a key piece of branding to entice your customers.

Imagine you are driving along the highway and you see a billboard. If it's well designed, your eye will most likely be drawn to a word or phrase, and an image or colours. Your book's front cover is like a billboard, you want it to POP!

Take a look at some of our recent covers. Below each I'll share my analysis.

The Human Reinvention Formula by Mia Munro

This book is all about how to reinvent yourself after life has struck you down.

What's the first thing your eye is drawn to? The bright colour splash? The human reinvention title?

When designing your cover, ask yourself, what do you want the reader's eye to be drawn to first? What do you want the reader's eye to be drawn to second? How about third?

Considering the priorities of what you want the reader to see and in what order really helps to create a compelling design.

In this cover, the intended "order of the eye" is the colour splash, especially red, then the title, then the sub-title.

Cut The Crap by Joanne Antoun

This book is about empowerment, healing, and creating the future you desire.

The first thing that POPS when I look at this cover is the photo of the author, even more so, the LOOK in her eyes. This photo EXACTLY conveys the energy of the title, *Cut The Crap*.

Should I put my photo on the front cover? I get this question all the time. Here is when I would consider putting my photo on the front cover:

- When a primary reason for the book is to accelerate your personal brand

- When you are the front man/front woman of your business

- You have an attractive, professional photo that conveys the exact energy you want to express through the book

- If you like being on stage/on camera/the star of the show

- If it would be a significant breakthrough in expressing yourself and making a public expression of what you stand for

It certainly is not compulsory to have your photo on the cover. I've written six books and only one of them has my photo on the cover. Often, the message of the book is more important than a glamourous photo. Here are some circumstances when I would recommend a text-and-image-only front cover:

- When the message is THE most important thing to make POP
- When you haven't quite 100% got the front cover photo you were hoping to get
- When you are more introverted, and your magic happens behind the scenes

The Freedom Warrior by Salena Kulkarni

This book by investment advisor Salena Kulkarni is written to show people how they can build a bigger life through alternative property investment strategies.

Notice the colours used here. The orange that is predominantly used on this cover is what I call "entrepreneurial orange." In design, every colour evokes a certain frequency of feeling, and can be linked to certain themes.

Brown—linked to earthy-based topics like farming, good for "salt of the earth" type inspirational stories

Purple—often used for mystical, spiritual type books

Red—often used for sales books as it emotes POWER

Blue—an authoritative, trustworthy colour, great for finance books

Orange—entrepreneurial, symbolic of innovation, doing things in a new way

Green—often used for health and wellness books, or books on humanitarian topics

Gold—often used to convey premium, high end

White—conveys purity, innocence, a fresh slate

Black—can convey premium, high end

Font Selection

The other thing to consider when designing your cover is font selection. Like with the colours, every font will convey a certain energy and frequency to the reader. You can tell a cheap cover when the font selected just doesn't resonate or match with the rest of the book.

Cover Design—Back Cover

The back cover serves an important purpose in "hooking" the reader in. Whether your book is listed in a physical bookstore, or an online bookstore, the back cover will likely be the second thing the reader sees, after the front cover. We divide up the back cover into three sections: the top "third," the middle "third," and the bottom "third."

Top Third—Headline and Back Cover Copy

The first thing someone sees when they flip over your book to look at the back is the headline. The headline is right up the top of the back cover, and it is the "hook" that engages the reader in the rest of the book. I like my headlines to be BOLD, CLEAR, and get inside the mind of the reader.

To come up with a great headline, ask yourself what is the reader constantly thinking about? What is the unspoken issue that is circulating in their life? What's the thing that they are thinking and feeling but cannot yet articulate?

If you need more guidance, one of my all-time favourite structures for a back cover headline is the classic "It's time to …" sentence structure. I first saw this structure used in Tony Robbins' *Money Master the Game*; I think he said something like, "It's time to take control of your finances" or similar. What I love about "It's time to …" is that it is bold, directive, and has a forward-moving energy which is always important if your book is offering people a transformation.

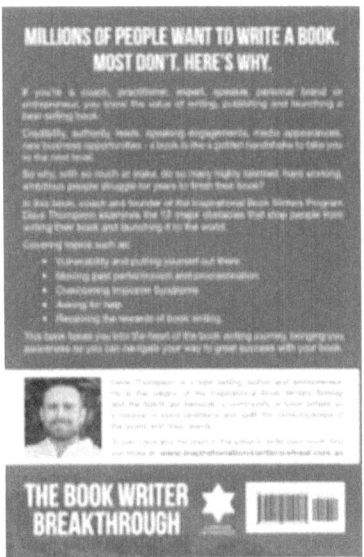

Photo: Back cover for The Book Writer Breakthrough

Still in the top third, but below the headline, is the back cover copy. This is the place to connect, inspire, and enrol your audience into your message. You want to speak directly to the reader, to what they must be thinking and feeling, to their fears, frustrations, but also their aspirations and dreams. Share your experience briefly so they know you know what you're talking about, and you may want to mention any social proof like awards or speaking on stage with other leaders.

Also common in back cover copy is the use of dot points to list what the reader will learn/discover or transform in the book. Typically I recommend three, five, or seven dot points, with five being my favourite number of dot points for a back cover. Dot points are particularly useful if your message or your style does have a logical component. That said, even if your topic is about the feminine mysteries, for example, I would still consider using dot points on the back cover as a way to easily communicate your message on a logical level.

Middle Third—Author Bio and Author Pic

These parts are important for communicating your authority and expertise. If one of the primary purposes of your book is to accelerate your credibility and authority, then you will want to get this right. Here's how we approach it.

With the author pic, you typically want a photo that is front to camera, eyes to camera. The middle third is a part of the back cover where the reader really gets to know you on a deeper, more intimate level, that why the eyes to camera is important.

With the author bio, keep it short to two to three sentences, and say who you are and what you do. You might mention some of the roles you play (for example, coach, facilitator, etc.) and you might mention the types of transformations and results you get your clients. If you get stuck, start with:

[Your name] is passionate about … [Your name] is on a mission to …

Bottom Third—Logo, Publishing Logo, and ISBN
We have a really simple structure for the bottom third of the back cover. On the far left, we use your company logo, or the title of the book. In the middle, we use the Inspirational Book writers logo. On the far right, we place the ISBN Barcode (International Standard Book Number).

Print-on-Demand (POD) Options
Print on demand book printing services allow you to print your book with no minimum order quantity. This is great because in the past, you typically had to commit to a minimum order quantity of 500 or 1,000 copies—which would represent a significant investment of money. If you didn't sell those books, you've just tied up your capital in boxes of books that would probably gather dust in the garage.

These days, print on demand facilities allow you to be agile, lean, and cash flow positive. You can print the EXACT number of books you need, and have them delivered to your door in usually one to two weeks. This is perfect if you run events and need books shipped to your hotel conference centre, or if you need bulk copies sent to one of your clients. It helps you stay cash flow positive because you can take payment from your audience for a pre-order of the book, then order the exact number of books you need to fulfil those orders.

Amazon KDP, Lulu, and Ingram Spark are some of the major players in the print on demand space. We have researched them all, and prefer the first two mentioned, for quality, customer service, and ease of use.

Audiobooks
The audiobook industry is booming right now, growing 25% year on year.[1] The chances are, as soon as you publish your ebook and paperback, you will have your readers asking for the audiobook version.

---

[1] https://www.forbes.com/sites/adamrowe1/2019/07/16/us-audiobook-sales-neared-1-billion-in-2018-growing-25-year-over-year/#29bbba1d6050

Audiobooks provide a brilliant medium to CONNECT even deeper with your audience. A book and eBook is fantastic. But audio, especially when you narrate (that's what we recommend), brings this whole new level of INTIMACY and connection and DEEP RAPPORT with your audience because they can literally HEAR and FEEL you through the words. Now think about this—the majority of audiobooks are listened to while people are in transit, either in their car or on public transport. So, potentially, their entire commute for a WEEK or more, to and from work, could be spent listening to your audiobook. That can only mean good things for your profile, your brand, and your business.

Go to https://bookwriters.kartra.com/page/audiobook to find out more.

Chapter 5
Launch Your Book to International Amazon Best Seller

Becoming a Best-Selling Author

For many people, becoming a best-selling author is a lifelong dream. Dreams of respect, accomplishment, having "made it" as an author, perhaps even being validated in your art—all of these are valid reasons why you would seek to write a best seller. Before the internet, very few people achieved this goal because access to publishing was so limited to those "sure bets" that traditional publishers were willing to take.

In the 21st century, thanks to the internet and platforms like Amazon KDP, becoming a best-selling author is so much more accessible. You don't need to have friends in high places, or jump through a million hoops to become a best-selling author. With some planning, strategy, and action taking, you can become a best-selling author even if you don't have a big list. This chapter will teach you how.

The Tall Poppy Naysayers
Before we proceed with the strategies and tactics for you to become a best-selling author, I want to address the tall poppy naysayers. When you rise, there will be some who want to cut you down. When you have a #1 Amazon Best Seller success, these naysers try to discredit your achievement by saying you gamed the system. I think they are completely missing the point. Also, they do not understand how the modern best seller system work.

#1 Amazon Best Seller—The TRUTH
As I mentioned, in the past, access to publishing was limited to what the traditional publisher gatekeepers would let through. Amazon didn't exist. Therefore, very few books could actually become best sellers because there was limited access and very few best seller lists. When Amazon entered the market in 2007, it opened up hundreds

of new best seller categories on its website. No longer was there just one best seller list—now there were hundreds. In addition to the best seller lists, it also began listing Hot New Release Lists in each of those hundreds of new categories.

In the modern era, Amazon has become the world's biggest global retailer of books! These days, if you're not on Amazon, you're nowhere when it comes to the book world. You want to be on Amazon—it is the biggest book retailer, and responsible for the lion's share of book sales globally, AND it has over 450 million customer credit cards on file, ready to make a 1-click purchase of your book! Amazon is clearly the place to be, and here is how it works.

The Amazon Best Seller Lists

Let's use this category string from Amazon's Kindle store to illustrate how the categories work. You'll notice that the sub-categories are all about niche topics, that all fit within the big category of Business and Money. The aim is for your book to collect all the available accolades.

An Example

Kindle eBooks > Business & Money > Marketing & Sales > Sales & Selling > Home Based

Sub-sub-sub-category: Home Based Businesses

This is the relatively easiest place to get a #1 Best Seller. Depending on which sub-sub-sub-category you are in, you might need anywhere from five sales to 500 sales to reach number #1.

Sub-sub-category: Sales & Selling

This is the next list you'd go #1 on.

Sub-category: Marketing & Sales

This is the next list you'd go #1 on.

Category: Business & Money

This is what we call a "category best seller." Over 90% of Inspirational Book Writers become a category best seller.

The Top 100 Amazon List
This is the Amazon list for the Top 100 books, inclusive of fiction and non-fiction. The Top 100 is a great list to be on because it gets a lot of traffic and thus a lot of eyes on your book. About 90% of Inspirational Book Writers hit the Top 100, many hit the top 50 and our top 10% hit the Top 25.

Regardless of where you end up, this is a huge achievement because Amazon has over 5,000,000 titles on its website, and many in the Top 100 are erotica and murder mystery fiction novels (which are super popular and sell like hot cakes!).

Although Amazon does not divide the Top 100 into fiction and non-fiction, you can easily work out where you sit on the non-fiction list by going to the Top 100 and seeing if there are any non-fiction books ahead of your book. Often, there's not—and so our Inspirational Book Writers also become the #1 non-fiction book on Amazon.

Hot New Releases
This is a list created by Amazon to highlight new books that have just been listed in each of the hundreds of categories on Amazon. These lists are a great place to be because some people are ONLY interested in new books, so Amazon sends these lists a lot of traffic.

Movers and Shakers
This is another list that Amazon sends a lot of traffic to. It features the books that have shot up the charts in the last few days. If you launch your book following the Best Seller Book Launch Strategy that is shared below, then you stand a great chance of making this list.

#1 International Amazon Best Seller
Amazon sells books in multiple marketplaces:

United States
Australia
United Kingdom
Canada

Spain
Italy
France
Germany
Netherlands
Japan
Brazil
India

Each country has its own set of hundreds of categories, best seller lists, and hot new release lists. This means you have the opportunity to become an international best-selling author by becoming #1 in multiple markets.

But What About *New York Times* Best Seller?

Sometimes people come to us asking about *New York Times* best seller lists, thinking that this is the holy grail. The truth is that to get on the NYT list, you need to sell about 5,000 copies in a one-week period, but it has to be through the NYT-approved channels. Many of the authors you see on the NYT lists literally bought their way onto the list by purchasing 5 – 10,000 copies of their own book. Yes, that's an expensive exercise, but if money is no issue, then fair play to you.

Comparatively, you can't buy your way onto Amazon's lists. You can't order thousands of copies, because Amazon only permits one eBook copy per account. Sure, if you sit there and create multiple accounts you could purchase multiple copies, but that would require a lot of labour.

And again, at the end of the day, you need to go back to WHY you started writing your book in the first place. For the majority of Inspirational Book Writers, your book is the vehicle to accelerate your authority, influence, and impact on the world. Why spend all that time and money chasing NYT, when Amazon is where it's at today?

Now, moving on to HOW to launch.

The House Party Launch Story

Sally's dad says to her mum, "Maybe we should go to France?"

Did you ever go to a house party in high school?

Do you remember the excited moment when Sally would come to school and tell everyone her parents *might* be going out of town for the weekend? Everyone gets so excited—there might be a big party! Everyone loves Sally's parties because last year she held a similar party and there was great food, music, everyone was dancing, it was a real hoot, and SO memorable. Not surprisingly, everyone buddies up to Sally, hoping to get an invite, *if* the party goes ahead.

Then a few days later, Sally's parents confirm they are flying to France for a week, and Sally will have the house free to herself. Sally races to school, and announces to everyone that it's PARTY TIME! The party is going ahead in three weeks. At this moment, the excitement and anticipation REALLY begins to build. The party is the talk of the school. Everyone wants to know who got an invite, and who is going with whom! The word of the party spreads like wildfire—first throughout the school (in like two minutes, cos, like, social media), then throughout the district as Sally's friends tell their friends, who tell their friends. Before Sally knows it, 5,000 people have clicked "GOING" on her Facebook event (luckily her parents are NOT on Facebook).

The excitement builds and builds and builds over the coming three weeks, as Sally does Facebook Lives with her friends where they talk about the party. She even brings on some good-looking football players to add to the social credibility and make the party an even more desirable event than it already is. These videos and cute selfies and snippets of what the party will be like serve to tantalise the party taste buds of the people going. To spice things up EVEN MORE,

Sally announces that she will be doing an amazing special offer for everyone who comes to her party—it will be just $0.99 entry! The people are SHOCKED. Sally's last party had cost $10,000 to attend and so being part of the magic for such a ridiculously low investment is beyond exciting.

Further, Sally, being the awake, conscious host she is, picks a theme for the party—AWAKENING. Having grown up with free-spirited entrepreneurial hippy parents, Sally is aware that what consciousness wants right now is entertaining events that are pleasurable AND have purpose, that are entertaining AND inspiring AND educational. This party is about more than just a good time—it has a deeper purpose to awaken the people that attend, to give them solutions to their problems, uplift their spirits, and ultimately, raise the consciousness of the planet.

As well as her global mission, Sally also has a personal mission. When she finishes school, she wants to be a speaker, build a business around her message, and travel the world, making an impact. To that end, she is also being quite strategic about the way she runs her party.

She is live streaming the launch to the world, so everyone who wants to be there is able to connect in. She has her team set up to give a virtual high five to every person who joins online, and a real high five to every person who attends in person! Sally is thinking about running a week-long retreat on her theme of AWAKENING for young people, right after she graduates in a few months—so she has an expression-of-interest form where people can register.

On the night of the party, everyone arrives and thousands of people are watching the live stream at any one time. Sally has a captive audience. She uses the opportunity to share her message of AWAKENING with the world, loud and proud. The guests hang off her every word, lapping it up with a gusto not seen since last night when Fluffy her dog licked the bowl clean at the end of her meal! People are hungry for Sally's message, and they want more!

The party ends with a literal bang—Sally totally ROCKS on the drums and she plays everyone a full-throttle goodnight lullaby (I know it's seemingly contradictory, but Sally just makes it WORK). The people leave inspired, in a beautiful state and ready for a good night's sleep. Sally is proud of herself. She just threw an awesome party. Way to go, Sally!

At the after-party, Sally is chilling with her closest friends, reflecting on the awesomeness that just happened. Her friend Dave informs her that her live stream was the #1 viewed live stream on Facebook that night, ahead of other live streams from Oprah, Tony Robbins, and Simon Sinek, amongst others. And not just in Australia either—the party live stream also trended #1 in the USA, the UK, Canada, and Germany! (All those German exchange students her family hosted over the years were tuning in to the party!) Sally is chuffed! She loves winning, and loves going BIG—especially when it's getting her message of AWAKENING out to the world. She pats herself on the back and says to herself, "Wow, that went even better than I thought!" With a smile on her face and happiness in her heart, Sally drifts off to sleep.

She wakes up the next morning, still in the feel-good, lovey-dovey vibes of the party last night. THIS is what it means to live life on purpose, she says to herself. After a walk on the beach and a delicious breakfast consisting of a dragonfruit smoothie, scrambled free range eggs, avocado, and a coconut, Sally gets strategic again.

She recognises that post-party, there are many opportunities. She must have spoken to more than a hundred people last night, and many of them wanted information on her upcoming retreat. Some said they wanted to order the recording of the live stream, so they could relive the magic. Others wanted her to throw parties for their people—invitations, open doors, and new opportunities were just streaming in.

Sally realises that the after-glow of the party has a finite time—but her reputation as THE GIRL that threw a party for the ages, well, that will never be forgotten. The media find out about Sally, and write articles about her as the Founder of THE AWAKENING PARTY. Everyone wants to interview her on their podcast! *The Morning Show* even interviews Sally, and that's when her parents find out! But by then, Sally's success is a runaway train.

Sally's dad turns around and says, "Maybe we should go to France more often."

The Best Seller Book Launch Strategy

I was embarrassed that I didn't know what to do.

Well, that's not 100% true—I did have *some* idea, I just didn't know the full story, which is pretty normal when you start something for the first time. Of course, I'm talking about the first time we ran the Inspirational Book Writers Retreat on North Stradbroke Island in 2014. I didn't actually have a set formula for launching a book—I only had a loose set of ideas about how to succeed online that I thought might work. I mean, I had been studying marketing since 2008, building websites, selling affiliate products, learning SEO, delving into everything Gary Vaynerchuk and Seth Godin had to say.

Gary V had taught me the importance of building personal brand, and how NOW was the time to build it. In *The Thank You Economy*, he spoke about how relationship-based business is the way of the future, and that transactional business will die out.

Seth Godin taught me about the value of art in the modern economy, and how to become so freaking valuable that no matter what the economic climate, you would be in demand. He taught me about the value of being uniquely me, weird and quirky and all! And in *Unleashing the Ideavirus*, he taught me how to turn your ideas into a virus that is easily "sneezed" out to others, spreading like wildfire. And I had just sold 500 copies of my first book in the first quarter of the year, so I did have "some" strategy to offer those first book writers.

It's just that my knowledge felt incomplete. I wanted a framework, something that was easily understood and could be implemented by anyone, regardless of the level of sophistication of their business.

Years before, I had watched Tony Robbins interview a whole stack of experts in online marketing. I trusted Tony, and so I trusted the people he presented. One name stood out to me—Jeff Walker. I researched Jeff, and found out that he is just a regular dude who has created huge success for himself and his clients, all through the framework he calls Product Launch Formula.

So I bought his book and the course (as you do) and devoured the content. I'm a rebellious creator at heart, so of course the first thing I did was mash PLF with everything else I'd been learning about marketing in the new economy, and create our own Best Seller Book Launch Strategy. Since 2014, we have run over 100 launches for our clients, and refined the method along the way. Here is the best of what we have learnt, about how to launch your book to success.

The Strategy

I told the story of Sally's AWAKENING House Party above because it illustrates the energy, emotion, intention, and strategy present in each of the four key steps in the Best-Seller Book Launch Strategy.

The Best-Seller Book Launch Strategy has four key steps:

1. Pre-Pre-Launch
2. Pre-Launch
3. Launch
4. Post-Launch

The Pre-Pre-Launch
Activate the Buzz

When Sally goes to school and announces that there's a party (possibly) going to happen, she is activating the buzz of the pre-pre-launch stage. This is an important stage because people love the excitement of finding out that something new is coming! There is anticipation and suspense, and the first movers will opt-in to follow you on the journey. Notice that initially, Sally was not selling tickets to the party, nor did she even have an official date—she was just sharing the excitement. This is what you can do in your pre-pre-launch.

Practically speaking, here's what you can do at pre-pre-launch stage of your book:

 # 1 Write a Pre-Pre-Launch Post and share to your social media and email followers.

*Note: extra points for an awesome photo ;)

#2 Start a VIP List

The moment you announce the book, people will want a way to follow your journey and get notified of upcoming launch news. That's where a VIP list comes in. It gives you the vehicle to be able to make your audience feel special, to build connection with them, while also thanking them for supporting you throughout the launch. You might have special offers, special not-included-in-the-book content or other downloads to offer them.

Technically, this can be a simple landing page with a name and email sign-up. Or if you're low-tech, just ask people to comment "VIP" on your Facebook post, and keep their names on a spreadsheet.

The big advantage of the VIP list is that by the time it comes to launch night, you will have a whole list of people who have opted-in, who want to buy your book. We have seen book writers get 80%+ of their VIP list numbers make a purchase of their book on launch night.

#3 Locate Your Resources

We take all our clients through a process called The Resource Locator. And no, this is not about locating natural resources—although it kind of is. What this is about is making a list of ALL the people, groups, associations, and organisations that you are connected with.

List out every single resource you have at your disposal to support you with the launch. An example list might be:

4,000 Facebook friends
2,500 Facebook page followers
2,200 LinkedIn connections
1,950 Instagram followers
1,800 email subscribers
Connections to X, Y, and Z influencers
Membership to A, B, and C Industry Associations or Education Providers

What media outlets do you have connections to?

Who do you know that runs a podcast that would have you as a guest?

What other resources do you have at your disposal? Time? Money? Knowledge? Skills?

Bringing awareness to all the resources at your disposal gives you a clear picture of where your strengths are and as such, how to best strategise the launch. For example, after doing this exercise, a leadership coach we worked with realised that she really did not have much in the way of an online presence—she had less than 1,000 contacts on social media in total.

But what she did have was EXCEPTIONAL in-person networks built over a 15-year career. She was connected to several coaching industry associations where she was really well known. As such, she deployed the Best-Seller Book Launch Strategy to focus mostly on emailing and phoning past clients, meeting up with them on occasion in person, and connecting into the people at the industry association that could help get the word out. Her 1:1 personalised strategy worked with great success on her book launch night, as her book went #1 Best Seller in multiple categories, all without the need for fancy tech.

Pre-Launch
Build the Buzz!

The pre-launch phase begins the moment you announce the date, time, and location for your book launch. For Sally in the example above, the moment Sally's parents confirm their trip to France, Sally is able to lock in the date, time, and location for her AWAKENING Party and thus her pre-launch begins.

Your pre-launch can be as short or as long as you like. Pre-launches can be anywhere from one to two days before the launch, to 18 months, with the average being three to six weeks.

When Apple launches a new iPhone, it doesn't do a pre-launch. It just goes "BOOM. Here it is." This non-existent pre-launch works because Apple has an established brand. They already have a following, and they know that their audience will be surprised, shocked, and excited when the new product launches. If you regularly post content, and have an established brand, this type of surprise launch can really POP for you.

I did a two-day pre-launch for one of my books, *Living Outrageously*, and it had great success.

On the other hand, we have had clients do pre-launches that lasted as many as 18 months. This lengthy pre-launch really worked for Relationship Expert EJ Love. EJ regularly posts content to her audience and for a period of 18 months, she would put the link at the bottom of every post, asking people to register for her VIP List. Come launch day in February 2020, she had a large list of people who had already put their hand up and BOOM! Her launch went off!

Here are the main strategies for pre-launch:

#1 Create a "Venue" for Your Launch (FB Event or FB Group)

Just like Sally had her house as the venue for her party, so too will you want to have a "venue" for your book launch. If you are doing a physical launch (more on that later) then obviously you will have a physical venue, but if you are primarily launching online, you will need an online venue.

The big idea is to create an online venue that is super easy for people to access. Facebook events, and/or Facebook groups are ideal because with one click, people can be part of your launch.

If you are doing a Facebook event, make sure you put the words "ONLINE book launch" in the description. Many people see the words "book launch" and automatically think it's in person, especially if it is an older demographic.

If you also want to build community around your event, you can start a Facebook Group for people interested in your book launch. The advantage of this strategy is that Facebook allows you to ask people questions before they join the group. This allows you to get a sense for what the people are wanting, and you can ask for their email address.

#2 Locate and Enrol Your Sneezers

In his book, *Unleashing the Ideavirus*, Seth Godin talks about enrolling "sneezers" to help you spread your message in an exponential way. Think about it. If I "sneeze" about my book, that sneeze will extend out a certain distance. I've got a good sneeze, but seriously, it's only me! If I enrol 20 friends who have the capacity to do a big sneeze, and we all sneeze at the same time, then there are 21 people sneezing simultaneously and the "sneeze" goes further, reaching more people.

A great sneezer for your book launch is someone who:

- You already have some sort of relationship with
- Already has a big following, or lots of connections
- Is aligned with your message in your book

We say aim for at least 20 sneezers for your launch. The great thing about being in the Inspirational Book Writers community is that you have the support of all the authors both past and present to support you at launch time.

*Bonus Challenge: In 2012, my friend Matt Kelly challenged himself to sell 10,000 copies of his new book on Outsourcing to anyone who would buy it. He made one call to Elance (now Upwork) and was just a signature away from sealing the deal with their marketing manager.

So my bonus challenge to you big thinking, revolutionary leaders is this—take out your phone. You have one phone call. And you need to move 10,000 units of your book with one phone call. Who do you call?

Several intrepid book writers have taken me up on this challenge, and while no one has yet moved 10,000 copies, we have had several success stories of bulk orders of 500 and 1,000 books come from this one simple challenge.

#3 Create Your Compelling Content Plan
You know that Content is King. You know that content can create a powerful, engaging story that enthrals your audience and has them high in anticipation of the launch of your book. See the below strategies for ideas for creating epic content in the pre-launch phase of your book launch.

#4 Document the Journey
The simplest, easiest, and most engaging way to create content for your book launch is to document the journey leading into the launch. Just document what you are doing!

If you submitted your final edit—document and share that!

If you received your proof copies—record an unboxing video!

If you are feeling a little nervous excitement—share that!

Your audience wants to relate to your human side, as much as your expertise.

#5 Countdown Posts
On the 12th day of Christmas ...

Remember the excitement as a kid of counting down the days to Christmas? Counting down the days to your launch can be really powerful, and it keeps people updated—especially if they are not online every day. You might do a 10-day or 14-day countdown, offering a sneak peek of the book each day—a quote, a photo of you, etc.

#6 Pain Point Short Videos
This will be especially transformational for you if you don't like being on camera! Pick the three biggest pain points that your book talks about.

For this book, I might pick the topics of:

- How to write your book in a week

- How to create a killer title and sub-title for your book
- How to become a best seller

And then, I'll shoot a short video for each topic, in the following Problem/Solution/Three Things format:

The video script might go something like this:

> *"Hi, everyone, Dave Thompson here. The problem most people face is that their book takes far too long to write, and therefore they don't write it.*
>
> *The solution is to write your book in a week.*
>
> *To do that, you'll need three things:*
>
> 1. *A solid Book Map Game Plan*
> 2. *Know how to tap into the Quantum Reality so you can write it in a week*
> 3. *Epic support from people that know the journey*
>
> *If you want to find out more, I'm launching my new book* Write Your Book in a Week *on XX date. Click here to join me!"*

#7 Prepare Your Offer for Post-Launch

Before you launch your book, it's a good idea to give some forethought to what you might like to offer post launch. People will naturally want the next step, so where will you take them? You might offer them:

- An invitation to join your free masterclass
- A strategy call
- A ticket to something else
- An invitation to a new group you are starting
- A meeting with decision makers

Imagine your book is already launched—it's out there, in the world, doing its thing—what is the next step for people who want more?

Launch
Shine!

#1 Special Launch Offer

Creating a killer offer for your book launch night is actually really easy. It's about getting three things right: launch pricing, creating urgency through limited time offer, and adding bonuses.

Launch Pricing

You'll notice that a lot of Kindle eBooks launch at $0.99. That's because $0.99 is the price point that optimises unit sales—and it's unit sales that count towards the Amazon best seller lists. I am a firm supporter of this strategy for a couple of reasons:

- $0.99 is an absolute no-brainer, red-hot offer. It's impossible to say no. Even if you are only moderately interested in the book, or have only heard a little bit about the author, you are still likely to purchase for $0.99 out of curiosity, or out of support for the author.

- A $0.99 customer is still a customer. Someone has still pulled out their wallet and made a purchase with you (well, technically with Amazon, but it's your product). Even this $0.99 purchase will "break the seal" for some customers. I have heard multiple stories from our book writers who had a customer purchase the $0.99 eBook, and then right after purchase a $10,000 training program with them. If your products and services are typically priced at the premium end of the market, and you release a low-cost eBook, your followers and clients will be SO excited that they can get a piece of your work for such a low price.

How to frame up an offer could be a whole book on its own, but needless to say, here is a few pointers for framing up your special book launch offer:

Create Urgency Through Limited Time
Emphasise the limited-time-only special—normally we would keep a launch offer open for three to five hours. This works to concentrate sales into that short time period and is more efficient for Amazon's best seller rankings.

Note: If you do have an international following, you might consider keeping the offer open for 24 hours, to catch every time zone.

Also note: You can extend the launch offer. We recently had a book writer who was still crushing it 24 hours into her launch—so we extended her to three days—she was still crushing it—so we extended her to five days. You do have that flexibility.

Also also note: Ensure you have a clear "end of offer" announcement and countdown to the end of offer. You will often get a 20 – 30% increase in sales in the last minutes or hours of the launch period, because the offer is about to go away and people don't want FOMO.

Include Epic Bonuses
It's pretty cool to get a lifetime's worth of wisdom in a book for $0.99. If you have bonuses that can go with the book, even better.

Digital bonuses can typically be included via links at the end of each chapter in the eBook, or at the end of the book.

Or, on launch night, ask people who purchased to email their Amazon receipt to your email address, so you can send their bonuses out to them.

Pricing Strategy After Launch
$0.99 is not forever. After your launch period, you will want to shift your pricing strategy. Here are some thoughts on that:

Remember those demand and supply graphs from high school economics class? Amazon provides us with a demand and supply graph showing the demand for your book at each different price level, for different categories of books similar to yours.

Here is an example for one of my books in the self-help category:

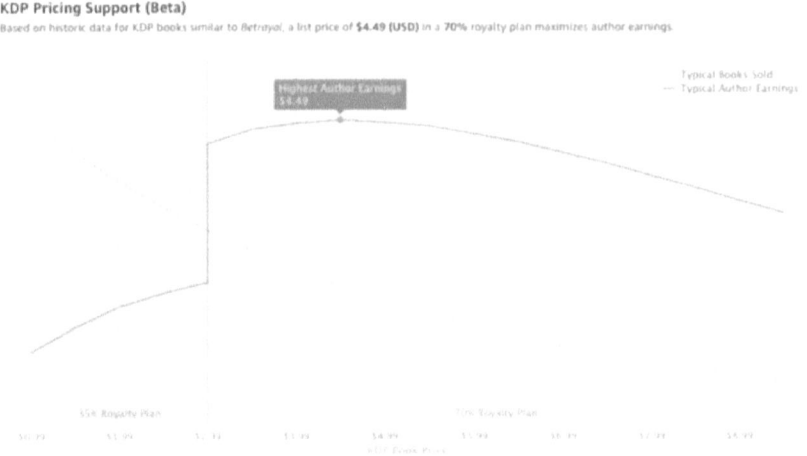

This particular graph shows that $4.49 is the price point to optimise author earnings, and most graphs I've seen recommend a price point between $3.49 – $4.99. Typically, we recommend our book writers price their books at either $3.99 or $4.99 after the launch.

Having said that, there are a lot of different factors to be considered. The three biggest factors we ask you to consider when pricing your eBook are:

- What price represents the value in the book? If you've included EVERYTHING you know, you might want to list higher because there's more value in the book.

- What price best fits your brand? If you've got a premium brand, you will probably want to go premium with your book.

- What price feels best to you? Always trust your gut instinct, and back yourself in your decisions. We can advise you, but ultimately you are the one to decide.

To give you context, Amazon's royalty structure works like this:

List price $0.99 – $2.99, and $10+ attract a 35% royalty payment

List price $2.99 – $9.99 attract a 70% royalty payment

(in Australia the 70% is available for books listed at $3.99 – $11.99)

Remember, your book is not there to make you rich off book sales—that is the old-school business model. The real profit comes from what comes AFTER the book. So, find a price point that feels good and makes sense for you and your brand.

A final note on paperback pricing—typically we would see pre-launch or launch special pricing at $14.95 – $24.95, perhaps with a free shipping offer. Then add $5 – $10 post launch for the paperback ($19.95 – $29.95), again based on the questions above.

We can do hardcover versions too. These cost more to print per copy compared to a paperback, but they can be awesome gift items for your inner circle. The average hardcover retail price we see is $34.95, and we have had clients sell their hardcover as a signed copy, gift wrapped with a personal message, for $60. When you sign it and wrap it, it no longer falls into the book category—it becomes a gift item—and thus you can charge more premium pricing.

#2 Facebook Live SHOW

The Facebook Live Book Launch SHOW is one of the central foundations of your launch. It's the hub for you to communicate with your audience, and direct them to buy the book, share it, and review it! Here are some things to think about:

Create a cool set

You want the SHOW to be interesting and engaging, so spend some time creating a cool set. This includes thinking about your background and lighting, and how you will frame the shot. It doesn't need to be super fancy, but just a little forethought can go a long way.

What to say

Within 30 seconds of going live, show the world your book! If you have a physical copy, show it to the world, or if not, post the link in the comments—right away! Then ASK, ASK, ASK. The launch period is all about flexing your ASK-muscle. Ask your audience to purchase, ask them to like, comment, and share your post with the book link.

When you start talking about the book, talk about why you wrote it. What inspired you to take the step to actually get it out of you, and into the world?

Talk about the mission of the book, and the ideas within it.

Talk about what the book stands for, and what it stands against.

Keep your content quite high level, mission driven and inspired—people will buy the book if they want more detail.

Your primary job on that Live is to inspire people to take action, purchase the book, share the book, and leave a review.

The SHOW might go on for 30 minutes to three hours—it really depends on what you want to share. You might also consider breaking the SHOW into two or three shorter segments, with an "intermission" in between. This gives you a chance to celebrate, eat, and reply to incoming messages, and it gives your audience an opportunity to purchase the book without fear they will miss any of your live SHOW. It also creates additional pieces of content which will remain current on social media for days after.

#3 First Fast Follower

Have you ever seen that YouTube clip where a bunch of people are having a picnic on the side of a green grassy hill? Then one guy decides to get up and start dancing. Everyone kind of looks at him a bit funny—who is this guy? Why is he dancing?!

Then 10 seconds later, his friend follows him, and starts dancing too. This causes the wildfire to take hold, and within 30 seconds, the entire group is up and dancing!

This wildfire happened because of the First Fast Follower (FFF). The FFF was the first person to follow, fast, and that triggered everyone else to get involved. The same thing happens online when you launch your book. Have at least one, if not several people in your support team to be your first fast follower. Their job is to buy your book, like, comment, and share everything you post on launch night.

Their actions effectively give permission for all those people on the sidelines to get involved, and trust me, for every like you actually get on a post, there are five other people who saw the post but didn't engage. Having FFFs is also excellent for the Facebook algorithm, which sees that your content is engaging and so is more likely to place it at the top of the feed.

#4 Amazon 5-Star Reviews

You want to get as many Amazon reviews as you can on your book's Amazon product page. For one, positive reviews are good for Amazon's algorithm in pushing you up the best seller charts. What reviews are mostly about, however, is establishing social proof. Think about it—if a stack of people have vouched for your book it makes it so much easier for a prospective client to purchase. Longer term, reviews are also essential pieces of social proof that you can use in book funnels, on social media, and in press release and publicity that follow the launch night.

The easiest way to get a review is to ASK. Make a powerful request of your audience: "Hey, guys, if you loved my book, I'd love it if you could leave a review on Amazon." If you want to, you can offer an incentive for people that leave reviews. You could send out a free physical copy of your book, you could run a one-hour masterclass for everyone that reviews it, or have some other bonus for anyone that reviews.

Aim for at least five reviews, and if you can get 20, all the better.

A note on reviews—Amazon only allows people who have spent over $50 with them to review products.

#5 Run Competitions and Special Offers
Running competitions is a great way to boost engagement.

Be creative. We have seen:

- Authors run freestyle-rap competitions around their book (think: best rap about the topic of the book wins a prize)
- Photography competitions where the best photo with the book (usually in some far-off exotic land, or the book in an unusual place)
- More straightforward competitions like "share the link to the book and go into the running for X prize"

For prizes, you can offer free signed copies of your paperback, 1:1 sessions with you or other people in your network who want to co-promote with you, or anything else you can think of that would be valuable as a prize.

To Landing Page, or Not To Landing Page?
A landing page is a one-page website that captures the visitor's name and email, before taking them to Amazon to purchase the book. This is a good thing because it allows you to capture visitors' email addresses; however, it does introduce a layer of friction.

Instead of clicking one link, arriving at Amazon, and making a 1-click purchase, the visitor now has to click onto your landing page, enter their details, be sent to Amazon, then make the 1-click purchase. It might not seem like much, but adding those few extra steps will reduce your purchase rate.

That's why we recommend sending the Amazon link out directly to your audience for the launch—no landing page. If you really do want a landing page, make sure it has great design, and a smooth user experience.

Post-Launch
Ride the wave! Making bank $$.

You've just gone BOOM out into the world with your book. Just like news, a book has a particular "shelf life" of relevancy. Here's how you can ride the wave of success of your book, extend its relevancy, and transition it to a permanent tool in your business for generating new business.

#1 Celebrate the #1 Amazon Success
You've just launched, and hit the Amazon best seller lists, potentially in multiple countries. Now it's time to celebrate and THANK all your followers and supporters who bought the book, liked, commented, and shared the book. People like to feel like they have contributed to your success and been on the journey with you—so share the results with them! This is excellent for social proof, and generates A LOT of conversations from people watching on the fringes. The fringe dwellers, often after seeing a successful launch, will feel inspired to come forward and connect with you, which then often leads to a sale.

#2 Offer Your Book for Free as a Download to Generate Leads
Post launch, your book becomes your secret weapon in generating leads and bringing prospects even further into your world and work. You can deploy your book in SO many ways, here are just a few:

Super signature at end of each post
Do you write content posts for social media and email followers? If you do, signing off every post with a "By the way, if you want a copy of my book, just DM/PM/click here/comment below" is a great way to get your book into the hands of prospects. Credit to Taki Moore for introducing me to this idea.

Email auto-reply
Do you have a permanent email auto-reply set up? If so, offer your PDF book on that auto-reply.

Email signature
Put a link to your book in your email signature.

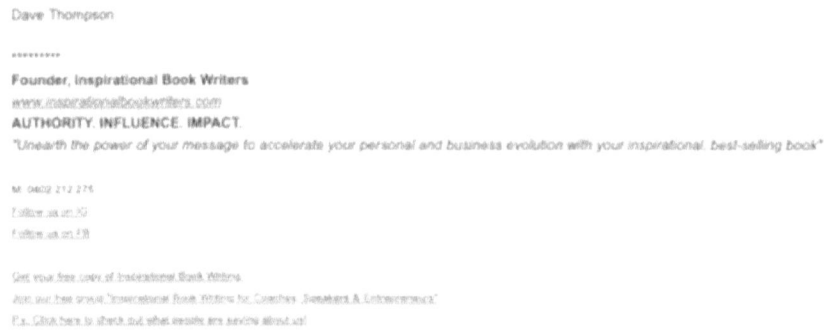

Instagram profile description

Pop-up on your website

#3 Offer Limited Edition Signed Copies

In *The Thank You Economy*, Gary V talks about how the modern economy is going back to a relationship-based model, where personal touch and personal connection is the key to success. One practical way to live by that is by offering a limited number of signed copies of your book. Writing a personal message to your clients, prospects, and audience inside the front cover is a great way to show them you really care.

When you personally sign, and perhaps even gift wrap your book, it shifts out of the category of being a "book" and into the category of "gift item." Once it becomes a gift item, there really is no cap to what you can charge for your book. For example, one of our book writers had a small fulfilment centre in her office. It was easy for her to personally sign, and gift wrap and ship her book. She listed her "gift item" of a book at $55 and was overrun by demand.

The keyword there is "limited." Several of our first book writers to do this did not put a limit, and ended up signing 500+ books! This is fine for some, but if you don't want to spend days signing books, perhaps limit it to 50 – 100 signed copies.

#4 Ship Bulk Orders

There are many organisations that would LOVE to buy your book in bulk. Whether it be a box of 20 books for a local business, a box of 100 books for a school, or 500 books for a big business, there are many organisations that want large orders of your book.

In your post-launch messaging, put out a message asking who would like a bulk order. You'd be surprised who will respond.

#5 Turn Your Launch Group Into Your Community

One way to build a business around your book is to turn your launch group into your community. If you had set up a book launch Facebook group, you may want to rebrand and rename that group as your community group post launch. Just make sure to ask permission from the group first.

#6 Getting Your Book Into Bookstores
When we upload your books, they get listed in ISBN databases around the world that can be accessed by bookshops. So if, for example, someone went into a bookstore with your ISBN, the bookstore would be able to order it in for them. In addition, you will find about six to eight weeks after publishing that your book has been listed on the online stores of many major physical book retailers. For example, my book, *Inspirational Book Writing*, is listed on the Dymocks online store, and other book writers are listed on places like Target.com

I know there is a certain allure to having your book on the shelf in a chain bookstore, but to get to that point honestly takes a lot of effort, and the royalties are super small (like $2 on a $20 book). If you do really want to go down that route, we can point you in the right direction, but it is not one we advise.

One avenue where our clients have had a lot of success is getting their books into local, independent (and chain retailers, for that matter) bookstores. For one, the royalties are usually much better (more like 30 – 40% compared to 10%, if that, with chain retailers) and independent, local bookstores are usually VERY happy to support local authors. Often, they will operate on a consignment basis, meaning they stock your book, and if it sells, they send you the cheque, and if it doesn't, they return your books. If you are looking to create the micro-celebrity factor in the local area that you service, this can be a great strategy.

Most of our authors have set up this arrangement by literally walking into the store, saying they are a local author, and speaking with the owner.

#7 Speaking Tour
If you have a big message that you want to share with the world, a speaking tour can be a great vehicle to get the message out. You can speak locally, regionally, go interstate, or even go overseas and around the world with your speaking tour.

It can be straightforward to get a speaking tour happening. Glenn Munso put up a social media post asking who would like to have him come speak. More than 12 months later, he was still touring Australia, speaking to community groups, helping youth get off drugs through health and fitness.

Design your speaking tour to suit your style. Colorado-based Ryan Parson launched his book in May of 2019, then toured around the state, speaking and empowering people with his book, *Your Money CEO*.

#8 Podcast Tour

The digital version of a speaking tour is a podcast tour. Podcasts have boomed in popularity in the last 10 years and podcast hosts LOVE to host authors on their shows. It's also a great way to get your message out to niche audiences. It also builds incredible rapport with prospects, because the podcast medium allows for a level of intimacy with the listener that is over and above other mediums.

You can do what Glenn Munso did and just ASK "Who has a podcast and wants to interview me?" and/or you can make a list of 50 podcasts you'd love to be on, and then reach out to the show's host.

#9 Media and PR

Mainstream media especially love the Amazon accolades. They lap it up, because it makes a great story.

Leadership speaker Heidi Dening launched her book *Her Middle Name is Courage* and became an Amazon best seller in seven categories, as well as becoming the #1 non-fiction book on Amazon Australia. She used these accolades to leverage her way into various media publications and mainstream media coverage, which then led to her speaking at International Women's Day in Sydney.

#10 Sell the Next Step (Post-Launch Messaging)

In your post-launch messaging, you want to stay engaged with your audience, and lead them to the next step with you.

Ask them questions like:

What have you loved about the book so far?

Who is already experiencing transformation from the book?

You can invite them to take the next step with you. This might be joining you for a free webinar or masterclass, joining you in a free Facebook group, in a new online course you are running—in essence, sell them/offer them the next step.

If your book has been written in a way that seeds a particular offer, then offer people the opportunity to work with you right after the book launch. You want to find the right timing between the launch and the next offer. For some, it will come right away, but usually we find it works best if you make your next offer (especially if it's high ticket) approximately one week after the book launch.

#11 Schedule a Rest
This is an often-forgotten piece of advice. When you launch, you are SHINING. Your star will be so bright, and it's your time in the spotlight—so enjoy every minute of the experience! But if you are introverted in any way, you will need a little cave time after the launch to decompress and rest.

#12 Relaunch Your Book in 6 – 12 Months
Your book is a foundational piece in your business. It's a tool you can use over and over again to attract new prospects, and so, relaunching your book every 6 – 12 months is a great idea. Some people may have missed your initial launch, or may have only just started following you, so relaunching your book is an exciting way to engage your audience and get your message out to people who did not receive it the first time.

If your book includes timeless wisdom that is universally relevant, you can relaunch your book every 6 – 12 months. You might launch it exactly the same way as you launched it initially, or you might try something new—like adding new bonuses, running a physical in-person book launch event (if you only did an online launch initially), or bundling your book up with other trainings you offer.

Remember, you have the option to do a revised edition of your book. This might include refreshing the content, updating information, and in some cases, designing a new cover to reflect your new branding.

*A word though on revised editions—sometimes it's actually better to write a new book.

#13 Physical In-Person Book Launches
A physical book launch is great for a number of reasons. Here are some ideas for how to think about your in-person launch.

Celebrate the Journey
You have just gone through this massive process to write, publish, and launch your book to the world. Having an in-person gathering to celebrate your journey with your inner circle is a great way to build even more rapport with your audience.

Social Media Content
When you have a physical in-person book launch, there is a huge opportunity for photo and video content that can then be shared all over your social platforms. This can be especially powerful if you have leaders in your industry present.

Conversations to Conversions
Smart marketers are optimising their marketing for "conversation" rather than conversion. They know that striking up conversation with a prospect is the way into understanding their pain, and then potentially leading them to a solution. A physical in-person book launch gives you and your team the opportunity to meet your prospects in the flesh and start a conversation, which then leads them to a conversion.

Many times, the conversations that our authors have with their book launch guests is just the conversation that opens the door to their next level of evolution in life and business.

Brand Boost
Why do rappers have such big brands? Because they throw EPIC parties! Your book launch party can be a talking point for months to come, and give your brand an epic boost.

Make It Personal
Do the launch YOUR way. If you like cupcakes, have cupcakes. If you like dancing, have dancing. If you like food by the ocean, find a venue by the ocean and have some great food!

Make It More Than Just the Book
You can couple your book launch with a presentation of you speaking, a performance, a guided meditation session, a dinner—whatever you fancy. Create the event you would want to attend, and feel free to charge people for attendance.

WHAT'S NEXT?

THE ONLINE BOOK WRITING INTENSIVE!

A virtual book retreat to Write Your Book In a Week

The Online Book Writing Intensive is a virtual book retreat to help you write your book in a week. It is the best group in the world for getting your book done, as you join Dave Thompson and like-minded coaches, speakers, entrepreneurs, and inspirational people from all around the world in a fully supported environment to write your book in a week.

You can participate from anywhere in the world via Zoom, and we run the event 3 times per year, usually in February, June and October.

To find out more and register for your place in the next Online Book Writing Intensive, go to https://bookwriters.kartra.com/page/OnlineBookWritingIntensive

WHAT PEOPLE ARE SAYING ABOUT THE ONLINE INTENSIVE

To find out more and register for your place in
the next Online Book Writing Intensive, go to
https://bookwriters.kartra.com/page/OnlineBookWritingIntensive

PUBLISH + LAUNCH

Publish A High-Quality Book Become a best seller

You've written the book!

Congratulations! But the hardest part is yet to come. Not knowing how to publish it has left so many manuscripts floundering in dusty hard drives, never seeing the light of day. What a waste! You could spend weeks and months doing it yourself, or save yourself the headache, and let us take care of your book project, so you can focus on what you do best.

Included is a full publishing package, including a copy edit, interior formatting, typesetting and layout, professional cover designs, eBook and paperback production, five proof copies, and listing on Amazon. Then, we coach you to launch your book to #1 Amazon best seller.

"It's like a service counter. You submit your work, IBW does its magic, then you get your work back for feedback. It makes the whole process so easy"—Stacey Ashley, author of *The New Leader*.

"It's a one-stop shop. It's fast and sexy simple"—Jean Sheehan, author of seven best-selling books.

Schedule a chat with us about your book idea.
https://bookwriters.kartra.com/page/PublishLaunch

FIND INSPIRATIONAL BOOK WRITERS ONLINE

Website: www.inspirationalbookwriters.com

Facebook: https://www.facebook.com/inspirationalbookwriters/

Instagram: www.instagram.com/inspirationalbookwriters

Email Dave directly: writeabook@inspirationalbookwriters.com

Join our free Facebook group "Inspirational Book Writing for Coaches, Speakers, and Entrepreneurs": https://www.facebook.com/groups/inspirationalbookwriters/

About the Author

Dave Thompson is a five-time Amazon best-selling author, entrepreneur, and the founder of Inspirational Book Writers.

The program is famous for taking coaches to paradise for a week to write their book, and publishing them six weeks later.

Since 2014, his WRITE—PUBLISH—LAUNCH methodology has helped over 300 coaches, speakers, healers and experts to publish their inspirational, best-selling books.

Known affectionately as "King Coconut," Dave is renowned for his island-style hospitality, fun, humour, results-driven focus.

To get in contact, email him at writeabook@inspirationalbookwriters.com

THANK YOU

Finally, I'd like to extend my thanks to a number of people who have been there for me and supported me and Inspirational Book Writers.

Davina Davidson—this ship really started to sail when you came on board. Thanks for being the best co-pirate anyone could ever hope for!

My parents, family, and Justine—for their love and support.

Taki Moore, Kiri-Maree Moore, Katrina Ruth—who all contributed key business strategies in the growth of IBW.

Jean Sheehan, Leigh Rourke, and Dr Suzanne Labrie for helping me get my inner game on point.

To all the IBW crew, contractors, editing team, formatting team, cover design team—thank you for being on this mission with me. Together we are creating big change in the world.

RECOMMENDED READING

WRITTEN, PUBLISHED AND LAUNCHED WITH INSPIRATIONAL BOOK WRITERS

A selection of our books:

Posi & Neg by Dave McCoy
The One Breast Goddess by Clare Elizabeth Dea
Sacred Mountain by Danijela Mijic
Bringing Life to Leadership by Michele Jones
The Entrepreneurial Hero's Journey by Dave Thompson

The Conscious Hustle by Dane Tomas
Infertility by Paula Tresintsis
This Time Is Different by Susan Santoro
God, Seriously? By Michael Shea

Culture is King by Jakub Wolanski
Vendor Management by Agostino Carrideo
Live Your Best Life by Michele Jones
Full Cups of Love by Tamara Burrell
Balance After Burnout by Dave Thompson

The Heart of Entrepreneurship by Samantha Riley
Just Do You by Benjamin Reeves

Clear Your Shit by Dane Tomas
Share Your Passion by Renee Hasseldine

Truthfully Heals by Tara Davidson

The Fat Ugly Beautiful Truth by Tamara Burrell

You Got This! By Cassandra Laverty
The World Actually Does Revolve Around You by Jodi Ashley
Anthea by Anthea Comerford
Love Yourself First by Joni B Hodson
Inspirational Book Writing by Dave Thompson

Tribal Unity by Em Campbell-Pretty
A Servant's Heart by Arpan Roy
The Art of Powerful Communication by Maria Pellicano
You Are The More In Your Life by Paula Tresintsis
Growth and Greatness by Runn Wild

The Jean Sheehan Story by Jean Sheehan
The Nutrition Code by Suzanne Labrie
Drugs Do Not Discriminate by Glenn Munso
Stop Ostrasing Your Negative Family & Friends by Leah Thomas

A Cosmically Juicy Life by Heather Joy Bassett
Some Things Never Change by Darcy Smyth

Life Rocks by Petra Jungmanova
I Became by Dane Tomas

I Did Something Different and it Worked by Nicole Mclellan
Built for Bliss by Trudi Bannister

The Integrated Man by Dane Tomas
Empowered Pregnancy by Sara Winchester
Invisible Work by Annie McCasland-Pexton

RICH! By Karen O'Connor
Living Outrageously by Dave Thompson
Create Your App & Grow Rich by B Kris
Unfuck Yourself by Zoe Swain

Dave Thompson

The Millennium Children by Jean Sheehan
Empowering the Millennium Children by Jean Sheehan

Unleash the Future of You by Kelvin Holliday
Unleash the Future of Leadership by Kelvin Holliday

The Art of Creative Business by Joyce Ong
The New Leader by Stacey Ashley
The Bridge to Animal Consciousness by Annie Bourke
Sex, Drugs & Mostly Yoga by Kara-Leah Grant
The Longest Foreplay by Aj McCoy
Secrets of a Sex Wizard by Dane Tomas

Her Middle Name is Courage by Heidi Dening
The Book Writer Breakthrough by Dave Thompson
Betrayal by Dave Thompson

The Freedom Warrior by Salena Kulkarni
Resilient As Fuck by Davina Davidson

On Track by Dr Nadine Sinclair
You Got This! By Annie May
Soul Truth by Leigh Rorke
The Art of Avoiding a Train Wreck by Em Campbell-Pretty & Adrienne Wilson

The Millennium Children Colouring Book by Jean Sheehan
BITE ME! by Jean Sheehan
In The Moment Coaching For Leaders by Jane Boardman and Sangeeta Pilger
The MUMFIT Book by Alison Simpson

Become The One by Ej Love
The Human Reinvention Formula by Mia Munro
Cut The Crap by Joanne Antoun
Levianthan by Sigourney Weldon
The Blue Diamond Souls by Zapheria Bell
From Hot Mess to Success by Georgina Noel

Notes

Notes

Notes

Notes

Notes

www.ingramcontent.com/pod-product-compliance
Lightning Source LLC
Chambersburg PA
CBHW021418210526
45463CB00001B/426